BARE KNUCKLE N

BARE KNUCKLE NEGOTIATING

KNOCKOUT NEGOTIATION TACTICS THEY WON'T TEACH YOU AT BUSINESS SCHOOL

SIMON HAZELDINE

LEANMARKETING™
★PRESS★

First Published In Great Britain 2006
by Lean Marketing Press
www.BookShaker.com

Typeset in Trebuchet

For my son Thomas who is already a very good "ghosteyater."
Tom - selling and negotiation will help you to get everything on
your list of dreams.

For my wife Karen who is one of the toughest negotiator
I have ever met - and I should know!

Contents

Acknowledgements

My wife Karen for her endless support, encouragement and proof reading – I promise not to write quite so many books in one year in the future!

The many customers, clients, suppliers, salespeople, bosses, business partners, joint venture partners, family and friends who I have negotiated with over the years.

For reasons of confidentiality I have changed the names of some individuals when they are mentioned in the book. You know who you are... and it's been a blast!

My publishers Lean Marketing Press – thanks for the support and advice.

Jamie Smart of Salad (www.saladltd.co.uk) for launching the Bare Knuckle Boot Camps in the UK.

The two hypnotists – Gary Outrageous (www.garyoutrageous.com) and Jamie Smart (www.saladltd.co.uk) for inviting me to be one of "The Three Hypnotists" – we should most definitely be banned!

Foreword

I'm famous for saying "Anyone can make £100 million" and as I have built up a series of successful businesses I have learned what it takes to succeed. You need self -belief and you have to get out there and have a go. There are also some vitally important skills that you need to grow your business profitably.

In the world of business you will often be negotiating on a daily basis and if you want to succeed you must be able to negotiate profitable deals. In the course of establishing and building a host of companies, including the largest privately owned health club operator in the UK, I have been involved in countless business negotiations.

Simon Hazeldine's 'Bare Knuckle Negotiating' contains powerful, practical and solid advice. This book cuts straight to the chase and will give you the inside track on what you need to do to improve your negotiating skills.

To make a £100 million you have to get out there and have a go.

So after reading this book put what you have learned into action.

Get out there and make it happen.

Duncan Bannatyne OBE
Duncan Bannatyne is the founder and owner of:
Bannatyne Fitness, Bannatyne Hotels, Bannatyne Casinos, Bannatyne Housing, Bar Bannatyne
www.bannatyne.co.uk

Preface

"In business, you don't get what you deserve,
you get what you negotiate."
Chester L. Karrass

Welcome To The Jungle!

It's a tough world out there – and it's getting tougher! Modern commercial life is very challenging with tens of thousands of businesses going to the wall every year. Businesses that do survive are finding that their profit margins are being squeezed, new customers are becoming harder to find, and more and more competitors are moving into their overcrowded market place.

Extensive consolidation is happening in most industry sectors as more and more local companies are swallowed up by national or even international giants. This consolidation is also happening on a global scale, with international companies swallowing international companies to form huge global multi-national corporations.

The consumer is more switched on than they ever have been before. They take advantage of tough conditions by driving hard bargains and are increasingly utilising the internet to compare and contrast pricing. When all of these factors are combined it all gets very worrying. It's rather disturbing, isn't it?

However, I didn't write this book to comfort the disturbed. On the contrary, I wrote this book to disturb the comfortable. This book is designed to be a wake up call for business people everywhere, whether working in a large organisation or running a one-man band. You have got to wake up and get real!

The tough conditions are here to stay. It's no good hoping that things will get better. They won't. Or at least they won't unless you do something about it. Keeping your fingers crossed and hoping for the best is not an effective survival strategy. If things are tough (and they are) then the only answer is that *you* need to toughen up. You need to continually improve and enhance your business and your business skills.

If you think about it for a moment, everything (in the material sense) that you want is currently owned or controlled by someone else.

The money that you want to flow into your business is currently owned by someone else.

The property that you want as your dream home is currently owned by someone else.

The equipment and services that you need to support your business are currently owned by someone else.

Therefore it is logical that you should spend some time to make sure you are able to get the things that you want from the people that control them, isn't it? That would be plain common sense. Unfortunately what is common *sense* is rarely common *practice*.

There are two vital things you must be able to do to prosper in business, and indeed life in general:

1. You must be able to convince people to take certain actions
2. You must be able to agree favourable terms for the actions to take place

In plain English these two vital things are:

1. Selling
2. Negotiating

Selling is all about convincing people to take certain actions – usually to purchase a product or service or to enter into some form of arrangement or agreement with you.

Negotiation is about agreeing the terms upon which the purchase, arrangement or agreement will take place.

If I can be blunt - my favoured approach – people who cannot successfully sell or negotiate are going to (metaphorically) have their legs taken out from under them by the people who can.

So for that reason I have written this book, "Bare Knuckle Negotiating", and its companion, "Bare Knuckle Selling". Both of these hard hitting volumes (pun intended) are designed to give you an unfair advantage over the competition. This advantage is the ability to successfully get what you want.

You must be able to sell and you must be able to negotiate. Where negotiation is concerned it doesn't matter if you are negotiating real estate purchases, attempting to save money on a new car, providing products or services to your customer's at a profit margin that allows your business to prosper or hammering a better deal from your suppliers. "Bare Knuckle Negotiating" will spill the beans on what it takes to negotiate better deals.

While "Bare Knuckle Negotiating" has been thoroughly and extensively researched it has not been dreamt up in an ivory tower. Everything you will read has been thoroughly tested and proven to work in real life negotiation situations where real money (very often my own) was at stake. These real life experiences of closing millions of pounds worth of deals have been blended with cutting edge research into the practices of world class negotiators to create the "Bare Knuckle Negotiating" process.

May I congratulate you on your decision to study the art and science of negotiation. It is a vital life skill and your decision to master it may prove to be one of the best decisions you have ever made.

Good Luck and Good Negotiating!

Simon Hazeldine, MSc, FInstSMM
www.simonhazeldine.com
www.bare-knuckle.com

What Is Negotiation?

"To be a good negotiator you have to be able to sell snow to eskimos!"

Clint Van Zamdt, FBI Hostage Negotiator

In the preface I discussed the two essential skills that you need to master to survive and thrive in business:

1. Selling

2. Negotiating

To be fully effective in business you need to have mastered both of these skills. The two skills go hand in hand and it is important to understand the difference between them, and when to do each. So first and foremost let's explore some definitions:

A Definition of Selling

Selling can be defined as establishing a need/want to buy, and then matching the benefits of your product or service to that need/want to buy. The benefits of your product or service and how they help the customer to get what they want are then combined in a reasoned proposal.

The entire process of selling is dealt with in detail in the companion volume to this book – "Bare Knuckle Selling".

A Definition of Negotiation

Negotiation can be defined as the process by which we pursue the terms for getting what we want, from people who want something from us. In essence it is a synonym for trading; for exchanging things we have that other people want, for things that we want from them. Or, "If you give me some of what I want then I will give you some of what you want."

Negotiation can also be defined as the process of bargaining to reach a mutually acceptable agreement or objective. It is a process where each party's view of an ideal outcome is adjusted to produce a compromised and attainable outcome - that to a greater or lesser extent - meets the needs of both parties involved.

Negotiation can also be defined as when two (or more) parties who are disagreeing, come together to attempt to reach agreement on some issues or issues. In this way the process of negotiation can be used to resolve disagreements, conflicts, strikes or any other similar event.

What Negotiation is Not

Most of us will have at some time watched what we may think is negotiation on television or in films. Whether it is Del Boy from "Only Fools and Horses", Arthur Daley from "Minder" or characters in a Hollywood blockbuster the scenario is all too familiar:

Character A: "How much is it?"

Character B: "Five hundred."

Character A: "Do me a favour! Five hundred? You must be joking! I'll give you one hundred for it."

Character B: "One hundred! It cost me more than that, you'll have to make it four hundred."

Character A: "Two hundred."

Character B: "Three fifty."

Character A: "Two fifty."

Character B: "Three hundred."

Character A: "Done!"

You may have experienced something similar yourself if you have ever haggled with a street trader for a souvenir to take home from holiday. In these circumstances you are expected to haggle! And that is the difference. Haggling over price is just that – haggling. It is not negotiation. Negotiation is far more than just haggling.

I am not opposed to haggling, I have done it myself on many an occasion. I once favourably concluded a very enjoyable haggle with a street trader entirely by electronic calculator! He didn't speak English and I didn't speak his native tongue so we conducted the haggle by typing our offers on his calculator. Even without the ability to communicate using a common spoken language we were both still able to put on a fine display of astonished and massively disappointed facial expressions at what the other person had typed as their price offer! I burst out laughing at his first price proposal, shook my head in what I hoped was a suitably "you must be joking" manner and typed my counter offer into his calculator. He dramatically threw his arms up in the air and adopted his best disgusted, "You rich bloody tourists don't know what it's like trying to feed fifteen children on a street trader's wages" expression. After much to-ing and fro-ing, walking off in mock disgust and a whole range of wonderful facial expressions from both parties (I'm still hoping for a call from the Royal Academy of Dramatic Art to invite me to teach my range of facial expressions to up and coming thespians) we concluded the haggle to the "satisfaction" of both parties.

However, this is not negotiation. For a start, it is very rare for any significant commercial transaction to come down to the issue of *just* price. Indeed to allow it to do so is not generally good negotiation practice at all.

Negotiation is The Trading of "Variables"

In the process of negotiation each party (usually) trades things they have for things they want from the other party. This behaviour can be seen in the classic tussles between employers and trade unions. The trade union want a pay increase of a specific percentage. The employer will only agree to this if the trade union agrees to some changes in working practice. It is very rare for negotiations to be confined to such clearly defined issues. Usually there will be a number of variable factors in play. Save haggling for times when it is appropriate to do so! We need to explore the art and science of negotiation in greater detail and leave the haggling to Del Boy Trotter!

A Trade Unionist's Definition of Negotiation

An experienced trade union negotiator once told me that he described negotiation by way of a metaphor. The metaphor he used was a room with two doors. The doors are at opposite ends of the room to each other. The trade union negotiators enter the room through once door and the company management negotiators enter through the other door. Negotiation is the process of deciding where in the room the agreement is completed. Is the negotiation concluded more towards the ideal position of the company or that of the union?

I have extended this metaphor by saying that if negotiation is deciding where in the room the agreement is concluded then selling is getting people to want to come into the room in the first place!

Selling is convincing the customer that they want your product or service because it helps them to get what they need. Negotiation is agreeing the terms on which the purchase will take place. This may include many factors such as volume purchased, delivery schedule and method, purchase frequency, amount of payment, timing of payments, advertising and marketing support and so on.

When To Sell and When To Negotiate

A simple rule of thumb to follow is:

Sell first, Negotiate second

The reason for selling first is that the more convinced the customer is of the benefits of your product or service the more they are likely to be prepared to pay for it! Sell first – it improves profits! On many occasions selling will be enough. You will be able to convince the customer to purchase your product or services without any negotiation taking place. If you allow yourself to be drawn into negotiation too early (as experienced buyers will attempt to do) you are weakening your position and missing out on the opportunity to convince the customer of the benefits that your product or service brings them.

Your Responsibilities As A Negotiator

Before commencing any negotiation it is essential to have clarity about what you want to achieve. Far too many people begin negotiating with a very weak idea of what their objectives are. So two of your responsibilities are first, to ensure that you know what your objective is, and second to achieve it.

Another responsibility is to think about any investment you make during the negotiation. I often encourage people to think about negotiation as a process of investment, and even to think about themselves as an investor!

An important responsibility of a negotiation is to get value for money that you "invest". It is good business practice to get a healthy return on investment. When you make concessions and agreements during the negotiation process you need to ask yourself, "Am I maximising the return I am going to get?" If it is your own money on the line and you don't get an acceptable return then you are personally missing out. If you are negotiating with someone else's money then treating it as if it is your own money helps to make sure you act prudently.

The final responsibility is to maintain relationships, both during and after the negotiation, on a positive basis whenever possible. If you are hoping to have any form of on-going relationship with the other party then keeping things positive is important. This does not mean to say that things won't get tough - they probably will. There is a difference between tough and underhand. Always seek a win/win outcome for both parties whenever possible. There are many good reasons for adopting this approach, which we will explore in greater detail in the next chapter.

There may be occasions when you don't wish to have any long term relationship with the other party and as a result you may be less concerned with the win/win focus. However on many occasions you will most definitely want to have on-going contact with the other party and therefore positive relationships are important.

With this in mind let us take a look at the subject of negotiation styles in the next chapter.

Negotiation Styles

"My father said: You must never try to make all the money that's in a deal. Let the other fellow make some money too, because if you have a reputation for always making all the money, you won't have many deals."

J. Paul Getty

Broadly speaking there are two styles of negotiation:

1. Competitive negotiation or "Win/Lose Negotiation"
2. Collaborative negotiation or "Win/Win Negotiation"

Competitive Negotiation

In competitive negotiation the focus is largely on gaining at the expense of the other party. It assumes that one party wins and the other party loses. This is why it is often referred to as "win/lose" negotiation.

At times our society seems obsessed with the concept of winning and losing. A common concept in modern society is that if someone wins, someone else has to lose. Perhaps the popularity of sport has something to do with this. Competitive sport, by its very nature, produces winners and losers. Only one person can win the gold medal, only one team can finish top of the league. And there can be rich pickings for the winners.

Sport is highly popular in society and I believe that, at times, it inappropriately influences people's thinking outside of the sporting arena. The sporting concept of duality – winning or losing – pervades our consciousness. If I win, someone must lose. If I lose, someone must have beaten me.

What is appropriate in the world of sport can be totally inappropriate in the world of business and in other areas of life. For example: sport produces winners and losers. If you lose at sport you are motivated to beat your opponents at the next available opportunity. Losers have absolutely no incentive to help others to be successful. In fact quite the opposite is true; losers want to make other people into losers so that *they* can be winners.

By its very nature this mentality assumes a limitation on what is available. It assumes that the only way to gain is at the expense of another. If you want a bigger slice of the pie you can only do this by taking it from someone else. If I get some more then you get less.

A game of sport takes place within a tightly controlled and constrained environment with rules and regulations. You are only allowed to behave in certain ways. The limitations are designed to produce a competitive environment that in turn creates an exciting sporting occasion.

The world of business (and indeed life in general) is far more open and flexible. There are endless possibilities and opportunities and choices. The competitive win/lose approach can limit the almost endless possibilities open to both parties involved in the negotiation

Competitive negotiation is often very transactional in nature. It comes from the perspective of a "one off deal". This style of negotiation will be characterised by the use of ploys and tactics (which I will expose in explicit detail later in the book). The aim of these tactics is to gain at the expense of the other party.

Parties involved in this style of negotiation will be on the look out for tricks and ploys. There will be suspicion. People involved may be inflexible and emotionally involved.

Some additional challenges that this negotiation style can produce are that losers have no incentive to help you to be successful, in fact, having lost they may wish to exact revenge if the opportunity presents itself. A one sided or lop sided "agreement" can plant seeds of resentment that may grow into big problems further down the line. A loser is hardly going to be motivated to uphold their end of the deal are they? In addition, if you win too often people don't want to play with you anymore!

Finally, this form of negotiation can undermine your credibility and integrity. If someone discovers that you have "got one over on them", that you have "shafted them" or "stitched them up", then they are hardly likely to want to do business with you again, are they? Indeed they may go out of their way to tell many other people about your underhand practices.

The competitive approach can be used for one off transactions but must be used with caution and with care. Using it can secure you the result you want; however, (as discussed above) it can also produce resentment in the other party. Should you ever need to interact with them again – beware!

Collaborative Negotiation

With this style of negotiation the focus is on ensuring that both parties gain. This is why it is often referred to as "win/win" negotiation. With this style of negotiation emphasis is placed on the needs and desires of *both* parties. Focus will often be placed on the importance of the longer term relationship between the parties involved. There will often be more trust and flexibility.

In a collaborative negotiation you are interested to properly understand what the other party wants. Information flows more freely as each party makes efforts to understand what the other party wants to gain from the negotiation.

In a collaborative negotiation both parties can gain. Time and energy is devoted to jointly solving problems and to resolving differences. Competitive negotiation tends to bring out or emphasise differences. Collaborative negotiation integrates differences. Collaborative negotiators have a problem solving attitude. They will consider how both parties can work together to find solutions. They will consider how any differences can be resolved by working together with the other party. You don't have losers in a collaborative negotiation. Successful collaborative negotiations only produce winners.

The collaborative negotiator will emphasise and use areas of common ground. The nature of the negotiation will be more open, considered and polite. Please do not make the mistake of thinking that collaborative negotiation is in any way a soft option – it's not! Collaborative negotiation can be tough. It can be very challenging to negotiate an agreement that suits both parties. It can sometimes be very tempting to slip into a competitive approach.

Collaborative negotiation can also take longer than competitive negotiation. The collaborative negotiator would see this time as being a wise investment in the long term future of the relationship between the parties involved.

With a solid win/win agreement both parties involved have a stake. Both parties will be motivated to make the agreement become a reality. The results of negotiated agreements don't happen automatically. It takes people to make results happen and if someone is happy with what they will get out of an agreement then they will be highly motivated to hold up their end of the bargain and to make the agreement work.

This motivation to make the agreement work is why collaborative negotiation is such an effective approach. Once a collaborative negotiation is concluded the people involved *want* to make the agreement work. They are motivated because they will be gaining. Both parties will be gaining and so both parties will be committed to making the agreement live.

Contrast this with the attitude and motivation of someone who has "lost" in a negotiation. How motivated are they to uphold their end of the bargain? Not very!

In addition this energy and focus on a synergy between the parties involved generates far more creative possibilities, far more choices, and far more opportunities. This can bring so much more value than could ever have been imagined at the outset. The collaborative approach is expansive – it opens up possibilities. The competitive approach has a more narrow focus and tends to reduce possibilities.

I have witnessed the negative effect of the win/lose approach many, many times. On one occasion a marketing manager for a branded manufacturer was negotiating a major contract with a distribution company who would warehouse and distribute point of sale material to thousands of retail outlets. The point of sale material was absolutely vital in maximising product sales.

I remember him proudly boasting in the office how he had, "screwed them to the floor on price" and how he had forced them to slash their charges to retain the contract. So what did the distribution company do? In order to make any operating profit they had to cut back on the service level they provided. As agreed with our "oh so clever" marketing manager they reduced the number of support staff taking telephone orders for the point of sale. They reduced the number of staff preparing the point of sale items for dispatch. They had been *forced* to do this. They were a commercial organisation and needed to make a profit. If they could not make a profit from the contract then why bother having it?

The end result was that service levels dropped, point of sale material didn't get distributed fast enough, the retail outlets became frustrated with the situation and the company sales force spent far too much time talking to angry customers who had been promised point of sale material that never showed up, when they should have been selling. The combined result was the loss of hundreds of thousands of pounds in sales. Hardly a successful outcome for either party! The marketing manager had not thought through his aims and approach, or the potential consequences, with the result that he very successfully shot himself in the foot.

There may be occasions when a win/lose approach is appropriate but I would advise you to think carefully about the possible consequences.

The Key Characteristics of Exceptional Negotiators

"...you need to be a good listener, see both sides of an argument, and be careful what you say."

Cary Cooper
Professor of Occupational Psychology, UMIST

Much research has been conducted into the profiles and behaviours of effective negotiators. Some of the key characteristics of effective negotiators are as follows:

Exceptional Negotiators Are Patient

The exceptional negotiator knows that sometimes things take time. When the need arises, the exceptional negotiator will take the long term view. They will be patient and pursue the more effective longer term objective. They will diligently pursue the robust conclusion, knowing that sometimes this takes longer to achieve. They know that in the long run, taking the time to build solid foundations enables you to build significantly superior agreements. If you have shallow foundations you can build, perhaps, a garden shed. If you have deep foundations then you can build a skyscraper.

Exceptional Negotiators Have A Win/Win Mindset

With reference to our exploration of the differences between competitive and collaborative negotiation, we can see that the win/win approach tends to result in more robust and lasting agreements. For this reason the win/win approach is the one favoured by exceptional negotiators.

Exceptional Negotiators Are Creative

Exceptional negotiators will work to develop new and creative solutions to problems; they will explore possibilities. By focusing on what is possible rather than what is probable, they are able to transcend deadlocks and generate synergistic solutions that will empower both parties.

Exceptional Negotiators Are Flexible

The exceptional negotiator will demonstrate a more flexible approach. In the same way that a river winds and turns around obstacles to get to the sea, the exceptional negotiator can demonstrate flexibility. The effective negotiator will make increased use of options and will consider far more variable factors than the average negotiator. As Dr Richard Bandler (the co-founder of NLP) has said, "One choice is no choice, two choices is a dilemma, three choices is a good start."

Exceptional Negotiators Ask Lots of Questions

Exceptional negotiators ask far more questions. They do this to gain information from the other party, to gain feedback on the other party's thinking, to keep the other party active in the negotiation and to buy valuable thinking time.

Exceptional Negotiators Don't Exhibit Behaviours That Have The Potential To Annoy The Other Party

Certain behaviours such as arrogance, the use of phrases or behaviours that insult the other party, their company or their products often backfire on the people who use them. These behaviours have the tendency to annoy people with the result that they retaliate. This rarely contributes positively to a negotiation.

Exceptional negotiators avoid using language that can annoy the other party. This would include phrases such as, "are you being serious?", "do you think we are stupid?", "we are making you a very generous offer!", "take it or leave it!", "can't you see my point?", "are you listening to what I am saying?" and so on.

Exceptional Negotiators Can Control Their Emotions

Although negotiations can become tense and at times heated, the more emotionally in control the negotiator the less likely he will be to make non-productive "attacks" on the other party or to make flippant remarks that may provoke an irritable response from the other party. In negotiation, the behaviour of one party can sometimes be reciprocated by the other party. An aggressive or attacking form of behaviour can often result in the other party doing likewise. In these circumstances the negotiation can spiral downwards into negativity.

Please do not think that the successful negotiator is some sort of unfeeling robot. Exceptional negotiators do share their inner feelings with the other party as this can help the negotiation process e.g. "I am feeling somewhat uncertain that I properly understand what you have said. This is making me feel uncomfortable. Can you clarify what you have said?"

Exceptional Negotiators Summarise Regularly

When I am training negotiators I will often say, "If in doubt – summarise!" As we will see later summarising helps to clarify understanding for both parties of the negotiation so far. It also helps to reinforce common ground and can buy you valuable thinking time.

So with the difference between competitive and collaborative negotiation established and with the traits of exceptional negotiators in mind let us now move on to looking at the process of negotiation step by step.

Negotiation Step By Step

"There are certain guidelines in negotiation, they are not rules set in tablets of stone...the negotiators have to have the flexibility to change. It has to be almost 'mercury like' flowing back and forth between the negotiator and the subject."

Clint Van Zandt, FBI Hostage Negotiator

This chapter's title promises to take you step by step through the process of negotiation. You may ask, "How can this be? All the negotiations I have been involved in have been pretty chaotic!"

It is true, in practice negotiations can get chaotic, messy and at times confusing. One of the reasons for this is that negotiations involve people. A very learned psychologist friend of mine describes people as "messy". What he means by this is that it is nigh on impossible to analyse the complex wonder of the human being in a black and white way. People just aren't that simple! As a result, negotiations aren't simple and straightforward.

The problem many people face in learning about negotiation is that they are hoping that someone will hand them a book that will tell them exactly what to do. They are looking for some sort of chess handbook for negotiations that outlines exactly what moves they should make in response to the other party. Unfortunately (or perhaps fortunately) negotiating just isn't that simple!

Each negotiation will be different. It will involve different people and different issues.

However, the good news is that underneath all of this will be some similar patterns. It is by understanding these patterns that you will be able to improve your skill as a negotiator.

This book will provide you with a handrail that you can use to guide yourself through the negotiation process. You will be able to know where you are, and where you are heading.

At this stage, I would ask you to re-read the quotation at the start of this chapter. Clint Van Zandt makes a very valid point that while there are some guidelines (which this book will outline) they are not set in tablets of stone. To treat them as such will be counter-productive as it would reduce your flexibility as a negotiator. Adopt the guidelines in this book as just that – guidelines. Use the guidelines, stay flexible, keep the negotiation flowing, and you will negotiate better deals.

So let us take an initial overview of the negotiation process, step by step.

As mentioned above, negotiation can get a bit messy sometimes, but most negotiations will follow a broadly similar pattern. The identifiable steps are:

Step 1: Planning & Preparing

While most negotiations may very well follow a relatively similar pattern, most negotiators fail to plan and prepare correctly! This vitally important step is often badly overlooked as the negotiators are too keen to get stuck into the action. Effective planning and effective preparation is the hallmark of the professional negotiator and we shall study this step in detail. For now, consider the difference between preparing (establishing what you want to achieve and gathering the information and resources you need for the negotiation) and planning (working out what you are going to do with the information and resources you have and how you are going to achieve your objectives). If you do not plan and prepare properly you can only react to what happens in a negotiation rather than lead it.

Step 2: Discussing and/or Arguing

Depending upon the subject of the negotiation and the people involved this stage can be a relatively calm discussion or a raging argument – or something in between. Whatever the nature of the conversation taking place, the purpose of this stage of the negotiation is to review the issue(s) and to exchange information. It is good practice to make every effort to understand the other party's point of view and to make sure that they understand yours. Some negotiators mistakenly push their point of view forward and do not take the time to listen and understand the other party's point of view.

Step 3: Signalling & Proposing

It could be said that each negotiation that you become involved in will always have two possible solutions – one that meets all of your needs and one that meets all of the other party's needs. In reality the final agreement will usually fall somewhere in between these two extremes. This final agreement will therefore be different from either of the two previous solutions. So, as a negotiator, you need to be on the lookout for signals, or signs of willingness from the other party to consider movement. You may also wish to *make* signals to the other party.

Signals are usually followed by proposals. A proposal is a suggested action, approach or process that one party in a negotiation makes to the other party. Proposals advance negotiations. Without them not a lot happens! Many people think that "you must play your cards close to your chest" when negotiating. While I do not, of course, advocate showing your entire hand to the other player, if no-one plays a card then there isn't a game to play.

Step 4: Bargaining

This stage of the negotiation is characterised by the two parties trading with each other. Variable items are traded so that each party can achieve their objectives. Again, many negotiators make the mistake of always playing "hard ball" and showing no flexibility or creativity. The key to effective bargaining is giving to get. However, you must never make a concession without getting something of equal or greater value in return.

Step 5: Summarising

As simple as this step sounds, effective negotiators summarise frequently. A good summary can ensure that your views are expressed correctly and can clarify that your understanding is the same as the other party. This can avoid misunderstanding later.

Step 6: Closing & Agreeing

As in selling, closing is when agreement to proceed is reached. At this stage you have a deal! You have agreed to proceed and have negotiated the terms upon which you will proceed.

Step 7: Making The Agreement Live

In my book "Bare Knuckle Selling" I make the point that *a sale isn't a sale until the money is in the bank*. In the same way an agreement isn't an agreement until both parties have successfully implemented what they have agreed to implement. To think it's all over after the final handshake is a mistake. The deal has to live.

For this reason, the superior results of collaborative or win/win negotiations (where both parties have a strong incentive to keep up their end of the deal) becomes obvious.

We shall return to this subject later, but for now please consider the vital importance of implementation and execution in making your negotiated agreements bear fruit.

It is perfectly acceptable, and indeed almost inevitable, that the negotiation will go backwards and forwards between the stages outlined above. For example, additional preparation may be necessary when you have understood the other party's needs more fully or a proposal may lead to more discussion/argument.

As you continue to read this book I will explain each stage of the negotiation process in greater detail and highlight to you the good practices you should incorporate into your negotiation and the poor practices you'd do well to avoid. In this way your skill and ability as a negotiator will improve – as will your bank balance!

The 2P Principle

Planning & Preparation

"If you fail to plan you plan to fail."

Abraham Lincoln

You may think I am getting somewhat above my station when I say that I think despite the fact that Abraham Lincoln may have been President of the United States of America, that he was wrong. Well not *exactly* wrong – just not 100% right.

I think his quotation should have said, *"If you fail to plan and prepare you are planning and preparing to fail."* Or at least in terms of successful negotiation it should. If you have not planned and prepared thoroughly - if you have not done your homework - then you will probably discover that the other party has the upper hand in the negotiation.

So why don't people plan and prepare for negotiations? Firstly, they don't know how and secondly, they don't have the time. With regards to the first point, by the time you have finished reading this chapter you will know exactly how to plan and prepare correctly for a negotiation.

And with regards to the second point, I am often asked how long people should spend preparing for a negotiation. My answer is, "It depends!" It depends upon how important the negotiation *is* to you. There is a difference between a one off negotiation about a purchase costing a few hundred pounds to a negotiation about a three-year multi-million pound contract. The amount of time required will vary depending upon the scale and complexity of the negotiation. If you fail to plan and prepare correctly for a significant negotiation then maybe you have not thought through your priorities clearly enough!

I do appreciate that the pace of modern commercial life may put pressures upon the time people have to plan and prepare for negotiations. However, ten hours planning and preparation is better than five hours, which is better than two hours, which is better than one hour, which is better than 30 minutes, which is better than 15 minutes, which is better than none at all!

Two of my best friends (who happen to be married to each other) are both professional buyers. One of them is Vice President of Procurement for a huge global organisation. I asked them to tell me what the most common mistake made by professional buyers was. They replied that the most common mistake was failure to plan and prepare correctly for negotiations with suppliers. Please note that these are *professional* buyers. They negotiate and buy for a living! They know only too well that they ought to prepare, but due to workload they don't manage to do the planning and preparation that they should. If professional buyers don't manage to do it, then you can be assured that many of the people you will be negotiating with won't either.

So if you want to be in a strong position in all of your negotiations you must make time to plan and prepare correctly. With this thought in mind, let us now explore the vital steps you need to take to plan and prepare thoroughly.

The Difference Between Planning & Preparing and Why You Must Do Both

I define preparing as having two important elements

1. Establishing the outcomes that you want to achieve as a result of the negotiation
2. Gathering the information and resources that you need for the negotiation

I define planning as determining your negotiation strategy. Planning is working out how you are going to achieve the negotiation outcomes you want. To do this you will be utilising the information you have gathered during the preparation stage.

Missing out on doing either of these vital elements may make your negotiation less effective and put you at the mercy of the other party.

With this in mind, what we will explore in detail in the next two chapters is a simple step by step process to prepare and plan like a pro. The steps we will explore are:

Preparing

1. Negotiation objectives – what do you want to achieve?
2. Power analysis
3. Shopping lists
4. Bargaining arena
5. Variables
6. Cost benefit analysis
7. Who will you be negotiating with?

Planning

1. Prioritisation
2. Information gathering
3. Key negotiation areas
4. Variables and opening positions
5. Concessions and walk away points
6. Negotiation style

If you would like to join me in the next chapter we will continue our journey to transform you into a negotiation superstar!

Negotiation Step 1: Preparation

"The more you sweat in training, the less you bleed in battle."

Martial Arts Maxim

The martial arts maxim above could be paraphrased to say, the more you plan and prepare for a negotiation the better the result. Even though you may not experience actual blood loss, if you don't plan and prepare well enough, you may very well experience some pain! It is unlikely to be physical pain but it could perhaps be the pain of losing money or profit.

Preparing Stage 1: Negotiation Objectives - What Do You Want To Achieve?

"Start out with an ideal and end up with a deal."

Karl Albrecht

Research into negotiation has frequently demonstrated that negotiators with a clear idea of what they want to achieve are far more likely to achieve the result they want. By contrast negotiators who enter into a negotiation with a weak idea of what they want to achieve will fare far worse.

In my book "Bare Knuckle Selling" I discuss the importance of setting what I call SMASH objectives. This process is perfect for setting your negotiation objectives.

By following the SMASH process, your planning and preparation will be off to a good start!

The mnemonic S.M.A.S.H. stands for:

SPECIFIC - MEASURED - ACHIEVEABLE - STRETCHING - HOLISTIC

SPECIFIC

It is important to know specifically what it is that you want. Your negotiation objective(s) must be stated in the positive: What you *do* want rather than what you *do not* want

Research demonstrates that explicit, specific and numerical (where appropriate) objectives are more effective in facilitating behavioural change. If you want to see improvements in your negotiation ability, then you must set specific and measurable goals.

You do not go shopping in a supermarket by making a list of all the things you *don't* want. You make a list of the things you *do* want to get. Do the same when setting your negotiation objectives. It is understood that the unconscious (everything you are not thinking about with your conscious mind at this moment) cannot process negative commands. In order to think of something you do not want, you have to think and focus your attention upon that very thing.

It is also theorised that the information flows into the unconscious mind almost instantly, whereas the conscious mind will take a few seconds longer to process something. So by the time your conscious mind has processed your goal to stop doing something (e.g. smoking) your unconscious mind has already processed the concept of smoking in order to make sense of the goal. Your unconscious mind is now focused on the very thing that you wanted to stop doing!

The "specific" step defines the result you want in a clear and unambiguous way.

MEASURED

How will you know when you have achieved your goal?

What will it look, sound, feel, (even taste and smell) like?

If, for example, you set a negotiation objective to "get a discount" and someone gave you a £1 discount on a £1 million order would you have achieved your goal? Exactly how much discount does "get a discount" represent?

Create a sensory-rich, specific goal. The more sensory specific data you can include, the more your brain has to lock onto.

It can also be helpful to set specific dates by which you will achieve your negotiation objectives. These dates will provide a reminder and create a sense of positive urgency. However, do not allow these dates to become a handicap by putting yourself under unnecessary pressure.

The "measurable" step provides clear success criteria.

ACHIEVEABLE

Is the achievement of your negotiation objective realistic for your circumstances and those of the other party?

The objective you wish to achieve has to be realistic. That is, it is possible for both parties to fulfil their responsibilities. I am a firm believer in setting ambitious targets (see below), however, can the person you are negotiating with deliver? And can you deliver? A deal that one or both parties can't deliver on isn't a deal at all!

The "achievable" step provides "can do" motivation.

STRETCHING

Is your negotiation objective challenging enough?

Research demonstrates that specific and challenging goals lead to a higher level of performance than easy goals.

There is a direct relationship between goal difficulty and task performance. The more difficult a goal, the better the performance.

While care should be taken to ensure that your negotiation objectives are challenging and not unrealistic (as described above), laboratory based studies have shown positive relationships between goal difficulty and performance, even in the case of unattainable goals!

In negotiations people will tend to underestimate what can be achieved; they set their sights too low. Be bold and set stretching objectives.

The "stretching" step provides the inspiration to become bolder and more ambitious in your negotiations.

HOLISTIC

Will the achievement of your negotiation objective(s) be good for the other party and for you?

It is very important that your negotiation objective has considered the potential needs of the other party as well as the benefit to you. Far too many negotiators only have their own objectives in mind.

If the achievement of your negotiation objective will benefit the other party then you stand the greatest chance of achieving it. It needs to be holistic for both parties concerned.

The "holistic" step provides a good win/win outcome for the negotiation.

Preparing Stage 2: Power Analysis

"You can get much farther with a kind word and a

gun than you can with a kind word alone."

Al Capone

It is not unknown for power to go to negotiator's heads. The thought of "crushing your enemies and burning their villages" Conan The Barbarian style, can get the primal male testosterone flowing. However, the role and use of power in negotiation will tend to be more subtle than nailing your opponent to the floor.

The pages of history are littered with power-crazed negotiators who savaged another party in a negotiation only to discover that they had actually shot themselves in the foot. Power is vitally important in negotiation and it is vital that you include it as part of your preparation.

In the early days of my sales career I was fortunate to be taken under the wing of a very experienced sales manager, Peter, who had extensive experience of negotiation. After having received a promotion I found myself working for Peter looking after a number of wholesale distributors who supplied a range of products to independent retail outlets.

I had not been in my new job for very long, when I paid my first visit to one of the larger wholesale distributors I was responsible for. My contact, a man called George, decided to take advantage of the arrival of a new wet-behind-the-ears salesperson and proceeded to savage me for an hour or so! George bluntly informed me that they knew they were a big and important customer, they sold lots of our products and if we didn't give him an additional 20% discount then he was going to send his sales force out, remove our products from his customers and stop distributing our products entirely. I had the sense not to agree to anything there and then and sought advice from my sales manager Peter.

Peter listened to me explain what had transpired and asked me to arrange a further appointment with the customer which *he* would attend. I arranged the meeting and Peter arranged to meet me several hours before the appointment so that we could plan and prepare.

On the day of the meeting I met Peter and we discussed our approach. I told him I was very concerned that the customer would remove our products from his customer and de-list our products entirely. I pointed out that they were a large customer and if we lost their business we would lose a huge amount of sales. The customer concerned sold approximately 10,000 units of our products each year and to lose that would be catastrophic! I also said that I knew that giving them the 20% discount George was demanding would impact our bottom line substantially. I told Peter that I felt trapped between a rock and a hard place!

Peter listened carefully to me and then after I had finished, smiled broadly. I looked quizzically at him and he smiled even more! Peter said, "Relax! We haven't done our planning and preparation yet. How many units of our product does George sell each year?"

"About 10,000," I replied.

"Okay, how much of his business does that 10,000 units represent?"

"From what the previous salesperson told me at least 20 to 25 percent of his turnover."

"Okay", Peter said, "So our products account for up to 25% of his turnover. So if he de-lists them he'll have to replace that turnover with other products, won't he? Now we know that we give a competitive discount already, so he isn't going to make a huge amount of extra margin even if he could switch his customers over to other products. He isn't going to benefit very much is he? In addition the reason his customers stock our products is because they sell well. We have several of the market leading brands. Why on earth would one of his customer's take out a market leading brand and replace it with something inferior?"

"But what if he instructs his sales-force to target our products for removal?" I asked.

"Well that's an interesting point. Firstly, we know that his customers stock our products because they are successful. So George's customers are going to take some convincing. I also know that his sales team are Okay but they aren't superb. Do you know what the maximum percentage of any supplier's products that I have ever seen a wholesaler's sales force be able to de-list?" I shook my head.

"About 15 to 20 percent and that takes quite a long time to do. You can't do it overnight. Can you imagine how hard it is to convince a satisfied customer to remove a product that is successful? Why on earth would he do it? So if we take the worst case scenario we could lose, at most, 2,000 units per year. If he stops selling our products entirely he is going to damage his business hugely, because competing wholesalers would be all over his customer base snapping up the business on our products."

As I thought about this I felt better. At worst we stood to lose 20% of our current business, not 100% as threatened.

"But Peter it's still 2,000 units!" I exclaimed.

Peter chuckled, "Simon, we aren't going to just sit there and let George do it. You know that and more importantly, he knows that. You have already established an excellent relationship with Bob over at County Wholesalers. He phoned me up to say how impressed he was with your approach and that he is very keen to drive sales of our brands. He wants to sell more of our products so that he can reduce his reliance upon his biggest supplier. He is highly motivated to work with us. And there's no love lost between Bob and George – they are fierce competitors. If George wants to play hard then we will support Bob to take sales of our products away from him. Bob told me if we give him some incentive support for his sales force then he is willing to sign up to increasing sales by 5,000 units this year. You aren't going to lose any sales on your ledger – they are going to grow!" Peter was now laughing at the look of surprise on my face. I had just had my first lesson in negotiation planning.

Peter and I spent the rest of the time discussing our strategy in the meeting. "They'll probably be mob-handed," predicted Peter, "If they are it probably shows that they are worried about the meeting." Peter was right, knowing that Peter was attending George had arranged for two more directors from his company to join the meeting.

Peter's final comment before we went into the meeting was to say, "If I step on your foot under the table, shut up and leave it to me." I was about to witness a master of negotiation in action.

For about half an hour I negotiated with George and the other directors, with Peter remaining largely silent, allowing me to take the lead. His presence along with the planning and preparation had boosted my confidence. As I refused to give in to George's demands, he began to issue more and more threats. Finally, he said that the meeting was finished and that he was going to immediately phone all of his sales force personally and instruct them to de-list our brands. Peter stood on my foot under the table. As arranged, I stopped talking.

Peter stood up, put his briefcase down in the middle of George's desk, opened it, put the paperwork he had been holding into it, closed the briefcase and extended his hand across the desk to George.

"George, it's a pity that you feel that way. I was hoping that we would be able to settle this matter in a manner that was beneficial to both of us. I will ask Simon to make arrangements to close your account with us by the end of the week." Then he stood there with his hand extended across the desk waiting for George to shake it.

For several long seconds there was silence. Then George, realising that his bluff had been called, flushed and said "Er... er... er... I... er... I... didn't... er... mean... to... er... for it to get... er... this... er... far Peter!"

Peter smiled, "Okay George," he said as he sat down, "Shall we have a sensible conversation now?"

Peter and I left the meeting having agreed that George could have a small increase in discount. However he could only have it in return for a significant increase in sales of our products. And the discount would be paid retrospectively at the end of the year on the condition that George achieved the sales targets we had negotiated. George got what he wanted and we got what we wanted. And I had learned some very powerful lessons about the role of power in negotiation!

So, what is power? My dictionary defines it as, "the ability to do or act", "influence or authority" and "an influential person, group or organisation". In a negotiation power is an elusive concept because its sources are diverse and numerous. I like to think that in a negotiation power gives one party an advantage of some sort over the other party. If you have an advantage you are usually able to conclude the negotiation closer to your ideal position than the other party's.

When I am teaching people about power in negotiation they get uncomfortable. The concept seems to unsettle some people, as though if we are pursuing a win/win approach that discussing power seems in some way crude or unethical.

The fact of the matter is that power matters in negotiation. It matters a lot! So let us explore some of the sources of power that may exist in a negotiation.

The power of size

The large number of spam emails arriving in my inbox week after week offering devices to increase the size of my manhood show that people know that size is important! I occasionally get paranoid that I am the only person receiving this type of email! And when my wife started to forward them onto me I really got worried!

Seriously though, the relative size or scale of the two parties in relation to each other is one source of power. For example, the smaller company supplying the large company. Other examples would be a company with a dominant or monopoly position. Questions to consider include:

- What percentage of their business are you?

- What percentage of your business are they?

- What is the relative position of the competition
  (both theirs and yours)?

The power of the current market situation

The current context that the negotiation is taking place within is another source of power. For example in the property market people will describe it as "a seller's market" or "a buyer's market".

Market conditions may also result in scarcity of a product or resource - in which case prices will tend to rise, or a surplus - where prices will tend to fall. A person with a warehouse crammed full of goods will approach a negotiation differently to a person who can't get enough products to meet a growing demand.

The power of knowledge and information

The more you know the more power you tend to have. The more you understand the market, consumer behaviour, your competition, and the other parties involved, the more you are better able to negotiate a favourable solution.

The power of time

Time is often a factor in negotiations. If one party has a need to meet an earlier deadline than the other party then this will affect the power balance. Recently I was negotiating a new car purchase on behalf of my Father. I ascertained (from wandering around the showroom and peering into the sales office when on-one was looking) that the end of September was the end of not only a sales month, but the end of a sales quarter. The very useful graph on the wall of the office (thanks for the information guys!) showed me that the sales team were a bit behind. Armed with this knowledge I was able to encourage the salesperson concerned to drop his price if we closed the deal before the end of the month. I knew that he needed some sales before the end of September. My father wanted a new car but we could have waited to purchase it. This helped tip the power balance in our direction and as a result we got a better deal.

The power of brands

If you are involved in negotiations that concern branded products then the power of the brands involved has an impact. If you are buying watches you are probably less likely to be able to haggle when buying a Rolex than you are when buying some run-of-the-mill watch. Branded products tend to command higher prices and higher margins for their manufacturers than non-branded.

The power of reputation

Some negotiators gain a reputation for being tough and ruthless. They can use this reputation to leverage an advantage in negotiations. When faced with the prospect of negotiating with such people, less experienced negotiators may feel that they are at a disadvantage.

The legendary entrepreneur Mark "The Shark" McCormack, who has been dubbed "the most powerful man in sport", says the following in his book "What They Don't Teach You At Harvard Business School":

> *"I have heard or read on more than several occasions that I am a 'tough' or 'hard nosed' negotiator. It's probably not a bad reputation to have precede me – people expect me to ask big numbers – but I prefer to think of myself as an effective negotiator, rather than as a tough one."*

So although Mr McCormack prefers to focus on his effectiveness as a negotiator he isn't oblivious to the advantage his reputation bestows upon him!

The power of status and title

In a similar vein to the power of reputation, inexperienced negotiators can allow themselves to become intimidated at negotiating with "the managing director" or "the vice president". The wise negotiator makes sure they are immune to the perceived status of the person they are negotiating with. I have it on good authority that even CEOs, Presidents and Royalty go to the toilet in a similar manner to the rest of us mere mortals. Perhaps imagining the managing director sitting on the toilet prior to entering a negotiation with him may lessen the perceived power his title gives him. I only hope he remembers to wash *his* hands before shaking yours.

The power of location

All good military strategists know that geography is a major factor that influences victory or defeat. This concept is well established. Ancient Chinese wisdom tells of thirty six secret stratagems of which one is to "Lure The Tiger Out Of The Mountains". In a military situation, luring the tiger out of the mountain means to draw your enemy out of his favourable natural conditions in order to make him more vulnerable to attack.

While we do not wish to *attack* the other party in a negotiation, we do need to be conscious of the power of location. People will tend to feel most confident in their own homes, in their own office or on their own territory.

Therefore, it is important to be aware of the potential influence of where you are negotiating on the negotiation. If at all possible, negotiate on your home ground or in a neutral location. This will give you a psychological advantage. If this is not possible, and you do have to negotiate at a customer's office, for example, then be aware that the other party may be feeling more confident, and make sure that you don't allow this to impact negatively upon how *you* are feeling. I have negotiated countless successful deals in customer's offices. Having an awareness of the various psychological factors affecting perceptions of power can in many cases neutralise their effect upon you. Later I will explore a number of underhand tactics or "power plays" that people may use to intimidate you. Having an awareness of these, and recognising them for what they are, will prevent you from being affected by them.

The two most important things you need to understand about power in negotiations

The first important thing you need to understand about power and negotiation – the thing you need to keep in mind – is that *power is all in the mind!* Feeling powerful makes it possible for you to *be* powerful!

We will view a negotiation through our perceptions. Our perceptions of the power balance between ourselves and the other party affect how we approach and conduct the negotiation.

The important thing to realise is that our perceptions are subjective. The amount of power we feel we do or do not have is entirely in our mind and in the mind of the other party in the negotiation. While I strongly recommend that you undertake an objective review of the power balance (or at least as objective a review as possible by a subjective human being) as part of the planning and preparation process, the fact remains that your subjective perception is far more important than the "objective" situation itself. If you believe you have the power then you have the power!

It is for this reason that some negotiators will indulge in various displays of power in an attempt to intimidate the other party. I will explore these tactics in detail later so that if someone attempts to use them against you then you can diffuse their impact by recognising them for what they are.

The second important thing to understand about power in negotiation is that you can enhance your power, and reduce the other party's power by planning and preparing correctly.

You can improve your perceptions of the power balance by planning and preparing for it. Some sources of power can be influenced and some cannot. You need to understand the difference between the two. By including power in your planning and preparing you gain a solid understanding of the factors involved and more importantly what to do about them.

Some of the questions you may like to consider are:

- Where does my power lie?
- Where does the other party's power lie?
- Where does the balance of power lie?
- What do I need to do?
    - What can I do to communicate my power?
    - What information do I need to communicate to the other party to demonstrate my power?
    - What information do I need to keep under wraps that might expose my weaknesses?
    - How can I reduce the impact of their strengths?
    - How will I handle the power of their strengths if they communicate them during the negotiation?

     o   What information can I gather before or during the negotiation to understand any areas of weakness the other party may have?

     o   How can I make use of these weaknesses during the negotiation?

Imagine that I am about to enter into a negotiation to agree a lucrative contract to provide selling and negotiation training to a company (let's call them Big Company Inc.) with a large sales force. The customer concerned likes what I have to offer (I have successfully sold him on the idea) and now we are to hopefully agree terms.

Notice the difference between my thought processes in these two contrasting examples:

1. Simon: "I am really going to have to be competitive with my pricing! Big Company Inc. are huge! There are over one thousand people in the sales force. Every single sales training company in Europe is after their business. I bet my competition will cut prices to the bone to get this contract. The buyer will have ten or more proposals on his desk. I'm going to be lucky to land this deal - I'm going to halve my usual day rate for this one because it's just so huge! They are even wheeling in the Vice President of Sales to negotiate. I've heard he's a real tough negotiator. This is going to be nasty!"

2. Simon: "I know I am not going to be offering the cheapest price. I never do. Big Company Inc. may be a large organisation and I am keen to get this contract, but I will only be able to do a good job for them if they are prepared to pay a good price. I fully expect a number of people will be trying to secure this contract. However from my research I know that most of them just haven't got what Big Company Inc. need. I am going to make sure that both parties get good value out of this agreement. It's interesting that the Vice President is attending. They must be taking my proposal very seriously. He wouldn't be attending unless they wanted to do this deal. I've heard he's a tough negotiator. That's good; we will be able to settle a robust agreement that's right for both of us."

Now notice the differences between these two contrasting thought processes from Big Company Inc.:

1. Big Company Inc: "If we don't get our sales training problem sorted out then we are going to be in big trouble. The last idiots we employed were next to useless. Their sales and negotiation training was so old fashioned it hacked off almost all the sales force. I'm so glad Jim the Vice President is coming to help me out – this one's going to be tough. E3 Group appears to be the only company who really understand what we want. I've heard Simon Hazeldine is one of the toughest, meanest negotiators on the planet. I mean he's even written a book called "Bare Knuckle Negotiating" – that tells you how hard he's going to be! He's going to take us to the cleaners. Bloody consultants! They bleed you dry. I have got to get this problem sorted or my neck is on the block. This is going to get expensive!"

2. Big Company Inc: "I like the look of the E3 Group proposal. It looks like it's what we need to solve our sales training problem. If we can agree some terms that suit both parties then E3 Group will get a significant contract and we get quality training. I've arranged for Jim the Vice President to attend so that we can get this deal closed as soon as possible. It's going to be fascinating. I've read Simon Hazeldine's book on negotiating and I know we will be in for a good meeting. We don't want to sign a deal to train our people with someone who can't negotiate a good deal for themselves! We want our sales and negotiation training to be the best, so we need the best. I am confident we can negotiate a deal that delivers high value for everyone involved."

If you compare and contrast the thought processes I am sure that you can see that in each case thought process number one is unlikely to lead to a successful deal! The negotiators are almost giving up before they even start! The second thought process will lead to a far more realistic and resourceful state of mind.

"Let us never negotiate out of fear,
but let us never fear to negotiate."

John F Kennedy

My karate Sensei used to tell me that the Japanese Samurai believed there were four ways of thinking that could result in you losing a fight:

1) Overestimating your own ability

2) Underestimating your own ability

3) Overestimating your opponent

4) Underestimating your opponent

If the Japanese Samurai got it wrong they might have lost several pints of blood and the odd limb. Thankfully none of our negotiations will have such consequences! However, learn from the Samurai and if you get in a balanced mental state where you are not over confident or lacking in confidence then you will maximise your chances of success.

By understanding the role of power in negotiation and by planning correctly you will negotiate deals and agreements that are robust, successful and lucrative.

Preparing Stage 3: Shopping Lists

If you want to have an efficient and effective shopping trip at your local supermarket then you need to compile a shopping list. If you don't have a list then you may end up walking out of the store missing several important items that you need. You may also end up with a number if items that you really don't need but that just seemed like a good idea at the time.

When preparing for a negotiation you need to prepare your negotiation shopping list. This is a list of the things you want to get out of the negotiation.

Sometimes, when I introduce this concept to people, they think that having a list will restrict their ability to respond to opportunities as they arise. "Isn't it better just to go with the flow?"

I am a strong advocate of being flexible and taking advantage of opportunities as they arise. This is good negotiation practice. As is making sure that you get what you want from the negotiation. In the hurly burly of a negotiation you don't want to miss out on any things that are important to you. This is where the discipline of shopping lists comes in. Have a list *and* stay flexible *and* be ready to take advantages of opportunities that arise. Compiling a negotiation shopping list is an essential part of negotiation preparation.

It is also very important to consider what is on the other party's shopping list. What are they looking for? How similar is their list to yours? How different is their list to yours?

It is important to differentiate between what someone genuinely *needs* from a negotiation and what they are initially *demanding*. As we will see when we explore "opening positions" later, it is good practice to aim high. So be prepared to do some work exploring what they other party is realistically looking to achieve.

Items on each party's respective shopping lists will become the key areas about which the negotiation will take place.

Preparing Stage 4: Bargaining Arena

The shopping list exercise will help you to understand what you and the other party are looking to gain from the negotiation. This process will also allow you to identify areas of common interest.

The collaborative, win/win approach to negotiation means that you want to produce only winners. Both parties must benefit. In order to do this you must identify and focus upon areas of common interest.

It is good negotiation practice to focus and expand upon common ground. If you can focus on areas of agreement then this sets a positive backdrop for creatively exploring ways to reconcile any areas of disagreement.

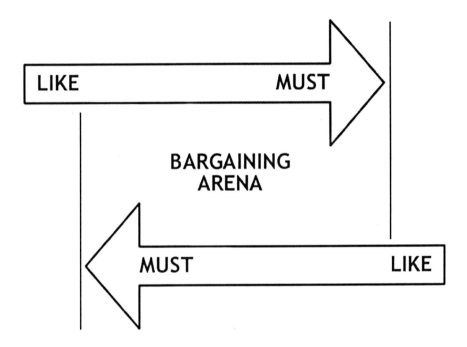

The term "bargaining arena" describes the areas in a negotiation where there is overlap between the two party's positions. A useful way to define it is to use the LIM process.

LIM stands for Like, Intend, Must. A parts of your negotiation preparation you need to understand your Like, Intends and Musts.

In reverse order LIM is defined as:

Must – This is what you absolutely must get out of the negotiation. These are your deal breakers. If you don't achieve these criteria then the deal isn't going to go ahead. This is sometimes referred to as your walk away point. If you don't get these needs met then you are out of there! If you achieve your 'Musts', then the negotiation has been okay.

Intend – This would be a realistic appraisal of the extra things you could secure as part of the negotiation process. It is an improvement on the "must" position and would be far more beneficial for you. If you achieve your "Intends", then the negotiation has been good.

Like – This is your perfect outcome for the negotiation. In this instance you have achieved all of your objectives – and more! If you achieve your "Likes", then the negotiation has been excellent.

Both parties will have Likes, Intends and Musts. The overlap between them is the bargaining arena. Your "Like" may perhaps exceed the other party's "Must" position. However, in-between these positions will be an arena you can bargain within. Identifying what this is likely to be is an important part of your negotiation preparation.

Questions to ask your self are:

- What MUST I secure as part of this negotiation? Why?

- What do I INTEND to secure as part of this negotiation? Why?

- What would I LIKE to secure as part of this negotiation? Why?

- What MUST the other party secure as part of this negotiation? Why?

- What does the other party INTEND to secure as part of this negotiation? Why?

- What would the other party LIKE to secure as part of this negotiation? Why?

- What are the common areas of interest? What is the common ground?

- What is the likely outline of the bargaining arena within which this negotiation will take place?

Having answered these questions will put you in a good position when you begin negotiating with the other party. One of the important tasks during the negotiation will be to test your estimates and assumptions about the other party's LIM.

Preparing Stage 5: Variables

A "variable" is something that can be traded as part of a negotiation. Negotiation can be defined as the trading of variables. When a variable is traded the proposition being discussed is altered in some way.

You enter the negotiation with your shopping list and the other party enters with their shopping list. You both trade variables to achieve elements on your respective shopping lists.

Some examples (this is most definitely not an exhaustive list) of variables would be:

- Timing of the deal
- Length of an arrangement
- Tailoring or customisation of the product or service
- Advertising support
- Marketing support
- Number of people involved
- Size of purchase
- Frequency of purchase
- Payment terms
- Endorsement
- Access to customer/consumer information
- Amount of display space made available
- Delivery quantities
- Exclusivity
- Geographical agreements
- Free stock
- Incentives
- Training
- Service

- Support
- Promotional activity
- Percentage of available business
- etc. etc.

The variables involved in a negotiation will, of course, be dependant upon the situation. However, one important point to note is that there are usually far more variables to consider and use than people think.

For example, people often allow negotiation to get narrowed down to "price". An important point to recognise is that it never, ever just comes down to "price". Here are just a few variable elements of "price" that you could utilise in a negotiation

- **When you pay** e.g. early payment, credit agreement, APR, deferred payment, retrospective payment, staged payments, extended credit, deferred price increase, pro-forma invoice

- **How you pay** e.g. credit card, banker's draft, cash, direct debit, standing order, cheque

- **What you get for the price you pay** e.g. extra features, support, service contract, training, marketing support, advertising support, delivery to one point, delivery to multiple points, quantity, quality, new model, old model, needs work doing, upgraded specification.

And believe you me, I have only just scratched the surface! There will always be many, many variables available to you in a negotiation. The more variables, the more flexibility, choices and options you have as a negotiator.

So to prepare fully, consider all of the possible variables you and the other party have at your disposal. This will contribute positively to your success in the forthcoming negotiation.

Preparing Stage 6: Cost Benefit Analysis

Having considered the variables that you and the other party have available, the next stage is to consider how much these actually cost each party. To get what you want in a negotiation you are going to have to trade variables. To do this successfully, you need to understand what it will cost and what you will get in return.

It can be helpful to think of trading variables from the point of view of making an investment. When you trade a variable in a negotiation you are making an investment. You must ensure that you get a good return on your investment. If you are investing in shares in the stock market you would put your money into shares that will deliver the highest returns.

So you must properly understand the full cost implications of any variables that are traded. When I am training people how to negotiate I discuss a concept called, "it's not just 5p".

Many years ago I made a mistake in a negotiation. I was negotiating with a customer and conceded an additional discount per case and did not get anything in return. The additional discount was "just 5p". It doesn't sound much does it? It's only 5p. However in the next 12 months the customer bought approximately 200,000 cases of the product in question. My "small" 5p concession ended up costing £10,000! And it gets worse! The customer was very successful in selling the product in question and in year two they sold nearly 250,000 cases. In two years my small 5p concession cost £22,500. I won't continue to calculate years three and four as the thought of my error still makes me cringe to this day!

I made two mistakes. Firstly, I did not fully consider the cost implications of conceding 5p. Secondly, I did not get anything tangible in return for the 5p concession which experienced negotiators regard as a flogging offence! There was nothing fundamentally wrong with making such a concession provided I secured a gain in return that was at least equal to, or preferably in excess of £22,500. It is true that the increased sales more than compensated for the lost profits, however I did not secure a robust enough return on the "investment" I made.

The other important factor to consider is the relative value of variables that you can trade with. Some variables will have a high value to you, but may have a low cost to the other party. And some variables that you have to trade with will have a high value to the other party and will have a low cost to you.

For example, if negotiating over a new car purchase, some variables that may be high value to you but low cost to the garage may include: metallic paint, free or extended warranty and servicing, upgraded specifications such as leather seats or alloy wheels, additional equipment such as satellite navigation, in-built DVD player, air conditioning etc. If you just focus on driving down the price you pay then you may miss the opportunity to get far better value for your money. It isn't just what you pay – it's what you get for your money that is important.

By the same token, some of the low cost to you, high value to the garage factors may be how you pay, when you pay, when you place the order, allowing a vehicle to be factory built and so on. If the garage needs to reach a sales target then your ability to close the deal within a few days could be high value to them. Or your willingness to wait a few weeks for your new car, perhaps allowing them to plug a gap in their production schedule, could be high value for them.

Thinking through the cost of variables that may be traded by both parties will allow you to make considered investments into the negotiation. Considering which variables are high value to you and the other party and, which are low cost to you and the other party will provide considerable leverage and at the very least it will stop you from being shafted!

Preparing Stage 7: Who Will You Be Negotiating With?

As discussed previously it takes *people* to make deals work. And it takes *people* to negotiate. It is therefore vitally important to understand who you will be negotiating with.

In the classic strategy text "The Art Of War" (written over 2500 years ago) Sun Tzu said, "Know the enemy and know yourself; in a hundred battles you will never be defeated." I will remind you once more that we are engaged in the process of negotiation and not warfare (although it can seem like a war sometimes) however Sun Tzu's advice to know the other party (and yourself) should be heeded.

As part of your negotiation preparations, think carefully about who you will be negotiating with. This will help you to plan your approach. Some things to consider are:

How many people will be attending the negotiation?

It can be somewhat disconcerting if you turn up for a negotiation on your own, only to discover that the other party is mob handed. I once looked after a customer who would insist upon having three people (two buyers and the Managing Director) attend every negotiation with me.

Now while I might take the fact that my contact would never see me on his own (I'm not that big and scary honestly!) as something of a compliment, if I was not aware that this would take place then it could have placed me at a disadvantage.

First of all, there is the psychological impact of being outnumbered. This could affect my perceptions of the power balance within the negotiation. Second, the other party could have an advantage in that while one of them is doing the negotiation, the others can be observing what is taking place and considering their options.

If you are going to be outnumbered in this way then you can at the very least prepare yourself for it. This can help to lessen the psychological impact. You could, for example, invite other people from your company to join you in the negotiation.

I would say that if you are taking part in negotiations with teams or groups of people representing each party then you must clarify each individual's role and responsibilities.

My experience with the customer mentioned above was that although they may have outnumbered me, during most negotiations they had not planned or prepared sufficiently and would often trip each other up during the negotiation. On one occasion the Managing Director burst into the meeting room halfway through a heated negotiation and told me that unless I gave them exactly what they wanted that two of our new product launches (which had a high profile media campaign running at the time of the negotiation) would be de-listed from his business immediately. After delivering his threat he glared at me in silence.

I had to work very hard not to laugh out loud. His business did not currently stock either of the two new products and we had no intention to approach his business to stock them for at least a year as we had signed an exclusivity agreement for the initial launch period with one of his competitors.

After a somewhat embarrassing few minutes the Managing Director left the negotiation (probably to issue threats to a few more suppliers) and the negotiation resumed. The two buyers that I was negotiating with could only apologise for the incident and I took the opportunity created by the interruption to calm the heated negotiation and make things more positive and constructive.

Likewise, I have on more than one occasion, witnessed a more senior manager joining on-going negotiations and lacking sufficient knowledge, making some ill considered concessions that ended up damaging profits.

Who is doing what?

The lesson is clear – make sure everyone on your team knows what they are doing.

I would recommend that you assign roles as follows:

1. **Lead negotiator.** This person is responsible for conducting the vast majority of the negotiation. The other people on your negotiation team are there to support the lead negotiator.

2. **Summariser.** This person's role is to regularly summarise during the negotiation. Summarising helps to clarify what is happening in a negotiation, it helps to focus on progress made and it buys valuable thinking time. A considered summary helps the lead negotiator to do their job.

3. **Observer.** This person's role is to keep quiet and to watch and listen. By not being immersed in the thick of the action the observer gains a different perspective and lots of valuable information that they can feed to the lead negotiator at breaks in the negotiation process.

What are the personalities and track records of the people you will be negotiating with?

It is very helpful to consider the type of person or people you will be negotiating with.

Any information that you can gather on them in advance will be useful. You can then use this to prepare and plan correctly.

For example, if you know the person is concerned with detail then you can expect them to go through your proposal with a fine tooth comb. If you have not prepared and planned for this then you will be at a disadvantage.

Any information you can get on their track record as a negotiator is useful. If they have a history of an aggressive pursuit of cut price deals then you can prepare and plan accordingly.

I would offer you four broad personality types to use to consider someone's likely approach and style in a negotiation. It's as simple as ABCD!

Analytical

The analytical negotiator is concerned with accuracy. They will usually be well prepared and systematic with attention paid to detail. They will make decisions based upon logical analysis. They will often be quite cautious about making decisions, and will focus on the practical aspects of the negotiation. The major weakness of an analytical negotiator is that they may over-analyse things and as a result, move cautiously and sometimes too slowly.

Balanced

The balanced negotiator is concerned with stability. They will usually be a good listener and will want to consider the implications of the negotiation on the people involved. They will make decisions slowly and deliberately. They often dislike major change and the impact of this on their own and others security. They will come across as being very supportive. The major weaknesses of the balanced negotiator are that they are slow to change and are very uncomfortable with conflict.

Converser

The converser is concerned with people and being recognised for what they do. They are usually very talkative and relationships are very important to them. They will often make decisions using gut feel. They dislike complex details and fear losing approval if they make a mistake. The major weaknesses of the converser negotiator are that they may talk to much, can be disorganised and as a result "wing it" in negotiations.

Dominator

The dominator is concerned with being in control and getting results. They are usually direct and decisive. They will often make decisions quickly as they want to get into action. They dislike people who try to control them. They want results and will get agitated if they don't get them. They fear losing control or being taken advantage of in some way. They will come across as being direct and at times impatient. The major weaknesses of the dominant negotiator are that they are impatient and do not listen very well.

I am sure that you can see how if, through a lack of preparation, you were to adopt the wrong style with the wrong person how things could go wrong! For example, attempting to give a "big picture" overview to an Analytical negotiator is unlikely to be effective as would attempting to go into extensive detail with a Converser. Pushing a Balanced negotiator into making a major decision quickly will result in failure as will trying to control and slow down the decision making processes of a Dominator.

After completing your negotiation preparation it is now time to move onto the second vital element – negotiation planning.

Negotiation Step 1: Planning

"Preparation and Planning Prevents Piss Poor Performance."

US Military Maxim

Having done your preparation, you now need to work out what to do with it. It is often said that "knowledge is power". I disagree. Knowledge is only power if you apply it and use it, otherwise it's pretty worthless. Therefore the major focus for your negotiation planning is your strategy – how you are going to achieve what you want to achieve.

During the preparation stage you will have worked out what it is that you want to achieve and gathered as much relevant information as possible. In the planning stage you are going to work out what you are going to do with the information you have gathered and how you are intending to conduct the negotiation.

As with the preparation stage there are some simple steps to follow to maximise your chances of negotiation success.

Planning Stage 1: Priorities

In any negotiation it is likely that there will be a number of issues in play at any time. If you have done your preparation correctly you will have completed your shopping list and will have done your best to fully consider the other party's shopping list.

The important thing to do now with these lists is to prioritise them. Imagine for a moment that after compiling your weekly grocery shopping list that you travel to your local supermarket. When you arrive at the supermarket you are greeted by the manager who informs you that due to stock shortages they are limiting customer purchases to five items per person. You now have to decide which five items are most important to you! In this fictitious example it is likely that you would choose essential grocery items (such as bread and milk) over non-essential items.

You would be unlikely to be leaving the supermarket with items such as organic washing powder, strangely shaped tropical fruits that you have never heard of, and ginseng flavoured ice cream.

In the same way you need to prioritise the things you want to get out of a negotiation and to consider the priorities of the other party. I am not saying that you shouldn't attempt to secure everything on your shopping list – you most certainly should. However, what are the most important things? These are the things to keep in mind during the negotiation. If you do not have clarity about this then you may conclude the negotiation with lots of organic washing powder but no bread and milk!

Having considered the other party's priorities will allow you to keep the negotiation focused on what they want to achieve as well. You are aiming for a win/win. If the other party cannot see how they can secure their priorities then they will be less motivated to negotiate a robust and workable deal.

Planning Stage 2: Information Gathering

Up until now you will have been making some assumptions and estimates about what the other party hope to gain from the negotiation. Hopefully this will be based on fact and experience. However it is important to check that you are correct.

A common fallacy in negotiation is that good negotiators get their position and point across first. In doing this they hope to shape the views of the other party. This may be so, but for a negotiation to succeed it must benefit both parties. Therefore it is vitally important to fully understand the other party's position, objectives, aims etc.

There is a difference between understanding someone's point of view and agreeing with it. Your aim is to gather information that will help you to secure a win/win agreement. You can only do this if you ask questions and listen carefully to the responses. Question and listen carefully to gather information that you can use to guide the negotiation to a successful solution.

How can you trade items on your shopping list for items on the other party's shopping list if you don't know what they want?

You must prepare the information you need to know and the questions you need to ask carefully. If you gather the right quality of information then you can often deliver an outcome that exceeds both parties' expectations.

Planning Stage 3: Key Areas

In most negotiations there will be a number of key areas to be discussed. The work you have done on shopping lists will help to establish the key areas that will form much of what is negotiated.

These could include areas such as price, quantity, timing, service, length of agreement and contract terms. When you have determined what the key areas of the negotiation will be, then you can move onto exploring the variables that relate to each key area.

However, before we do this, it is important to stress that one of the key characteristics of skilled negotiators is their flexibility. A common mistake that people make as part of their planning is to spend too much time on the order in which the key issues will be discussed.

You may spend quite a lot of time deciding that you want to discuss the timing of the agreement, before moving onto how long the agreement will last, before considering the quantity of goods involved. Your carefully constructed plans are then scuppered by the other party's refusal to discuss the timing of the agreement until you are able to commit to the quantity of goods involved.

It may be possible in some negotiations to handle a number of key areas in a pre-planned sequence. However what is more common is for some (or all) of the key elements to be interrelated in some way. For example, I may wish to hold back from making a commitment to a quantity of goods as my commitment may rest upon the length of agreement that I can secure. This in turn is affected by how soon I can move the stock holding I have from my current supplier through my distribution network.

The wise negotiator will consider each key area in isolation and then consider its interrelationship with other key areas. This allows you to respond effectively during the negotiation process.

I am not saying that you should not consider your preferred sequence to discuss each key area. During the negotiation you can propose this as a way of conducting the negotiation. If you get your way then good! However, if the other party wants to discuss the key areas in a different way then you can flex and adapt your approach if you choose to do so.

One thing to be aware of is that some negotiators will use issues such as the way the discussion should be sequenced as a way of imposing their will upon the negotiation. This can have the psychological effect of shifting the power balance in their direction, as they are controlling how the negotiation is conducted. Remember, power is often all in your mind and you should not overlook the subtle effect of such actions upon your power perceptions.

An essential part of your key area planning is to again revisit areas of common interest that have been suggested by your shopping list preparation. Where do you have shared interests, shared problems or shared challenges with the other party? Focusing on these at an early stage in the negotiation (and indeed focusing on them repeatedly and frequently during the negotiation) will help you to craft the robust win/win agreements that will deliver profitable results on an on-going basis.

Planning Stage 4: Variables & Opening Positions

Having established what you believe the key areas of the negotiation are likely to be, you can then plan how to utilise the variable factors that you considered as part of step five of your preparation.

For each key area in a negotiation there will be variable factors. All of these variables provide options you can explore during the negotiation. Good negotiators are flexible negotiators and the more variable factors you have to play with the better.

By way of example let us explore a scenario where I am negotiating with a conference organiser about my speaking fee. This negotiation could get narrowed down to how much money they will pay me to turn up and deliver a keynote speech.

Let us assume that having sold the organiser on having me as their keynote speaker and ascertaining what budget they have for the event that I have quoted a figure of £5000. The organiser has expressed a concern that this amount is "far too expensive". We could get locked into a haggle over the £5000 fee and then we are going to go backwards and forwards with the organiser trying to drive the price down, and me trying to drive the price up.

Exploring some variable factors could help to secure a valuable win/win for both myself and the conference organiser.

If I explore what items he has on his shopping list I may discover that he has been tasked with making the event very memorable. He wants the audience to go home with a lot of added value that they didn't expect, as they want to gain repeat business by getting the attendees to attend a subsequent conference. He needs to cover overheads, promotional costs and so on.

On my shopping list is, of course, my fee. However, what I am really concerned about is how much money I make from the event. Some of the money that I receive can come from other avenues than just the fee payment. And in addition to just the fee there are a number of other things that I am interested to secure.

For example, I can make money from selling my books and other products at the event. If the organiser will provide me with a space in the conference hall where I can promote my products then I can make money that way. There are more variables around this product area. I could cut the organiser in on a slice of the profits. I could supply some of my products free of charge as prizes or incentives. I could agree to make one of my tips books free to each audience member. As my tips books will contain adverts for my more expensive products then this would have other advantages for me anyway.

I could propose that the organiser makes contact details of all of the people attending available to me so that I could add them to my database.

If the organiser is recording or videoing the event then I could ask for a copy that I could then turn into a product for future sale. Or I could ask to record the event myself and then offer it to the audience as a product.

I could offer to add value by perhaps offering a workshop session at the event in addition to just delivering my keynote speech. I am - after all - going to be there anyway.

I could negotiate a different fee structure if the organiser agrees to book me at the future event he is organising.

I could offer to market the event to my own database in return for a commission on each person who attends as a result.

As I am sure you can see there are many, many possible variables around the key area of my fee! I have only scratched the surface of the many variables but I hope that this has given you some food for thought.

Opening positions

When, during the negotiation process, you move into the bargaining stage you will need to have considered your opening position. This is where you will communicate your initial aspiration and the other party will communicate theirs.

There are some things to bear in mind when planning your approach. Sometimes negotiations will circle around and around without making any real progress. This can be due to each party's reluctance to make the opening move.

It is indeed good negotiation practice to let the other party make their opening proposal first. This can give you valuable information which can prove useful before you state your opening position. It is therefore good to plan an approach to encourage the other party to state their opening position.

However, if the other party will not state their opening position then you need to have planned your approach. In a game of cards if no-one plays a card then there is no game to play. It is the same in a negotiation; if no-one is prepared to state their opening position then this can result in the endless circling around mentioned earlier.

To get things moving you may have to be prepared to make the opening move. If you do so then the advice is to aim high. However aiming high does not mean being unrealistic. A considered and credible high opening position communicates confidence to the other party. A good opening position can lower the other party's expectations about what is possible, and give you room to make concessions and still end up with a profitable outcome.

It is more common for negotiators to err too far on the side of caution and open at a lower position than they could do. If the other party sense this caution they may push even harder! So have confidence and aim high.

However aiming *too* high can damage your credibility and cause you to have to make some huge concessions in order to secure a deal that will be workable. Making huge concessions, as we will see later, can be harmful to the final outcome. In addition, if you have to negotiate with the same person again you will have inadvertently taught them to ignore your opening offer! So do aim high but not at a level that you cannot sensibly negotiate from.

When I was buying double glazing for my house I invited four companies to bid for the business. My plan was to put the four of them in a competitive situation with each other and drive the price of the double glazing down. The only down side to my plan was having to put up with presentations from *four* double glazing salespeople!

Please don't misunderstand me, I think double glazing is an excellent product – I wanted it fitted in my house. The problem is, that for some reason, far too many double glazing companies insist on using manipulative sales tactics and ridiculous negotiation ploys to secure business.

If they insist on behaving like this then I am sure that you can understand why I, as a professional persuader and negotiator, enjoy having some sport with them! More of this later! In the course of buying my double glazing a common approach that I observed was for the salesperson to offer an initial price that was ridiculously high. I believe this is done to make any subsequent "special offer prices" seem good value for money. This didn't work with me! These over-inflated prices just made the salespeople look like amateurs and dare I say, lambs to the slaughter. Selling and negotiating like this is not my preferred or recommended approach but if people insist upon behaving stupidly then you can hardly blame me for taking advantage, can you?

In stage four of the planning process you gave some thought to the bargaining arena. Using this information a strong and credible opening position would be to open slightly above your LIKE and slightly below the other party's MUST. This means that the other party have some motivation to negotiate (they can see that there is a chance that they can negotiate a workable deal) whilst you have started to manage their expectations about what you will accept.

Planning Stage 5: Concessions & Walk Away Points

People sometimes make the mistake that giving anything away in a negotiation is a sign of weakness. They are wrong! Good negotiators understand that you have to give to get. If there is no trading then there is no progress. By making considered and conditional concessions you will always get something - often something of higher value - in return. This is good negotiation practice. What is poor negotiation practice is to concede something without getting something in return.

This is so important that I would like you to stand up, place your hand on your heart and solemnly state out loud (in a deep and serious sort of voice):

> *"I do solemnly swear that I will never again give anything away in a negotiation without securing something of equal or greater value in return!"*

Thanks for joining in! If you are reading this book on a bus, train or plane I hope that everyone has stopped staring at you by now!

Having firmly established the "give to get" principle, you need to think through what you can concede and what you want in return. Re-visit your thinking around shopping lists, variable factors and the cost associated with these. You will then be in a position to make considered concessions in order to get the things you want out of the negotiation.

The subject of walk away points also needs to be considered fully before you start negotiating. A walk away point is, as the name implies, the point at which you walk away from the negotiation. That is, where the negotiation has reached a stage where it is no longer viable for one party or indeed for both parties.

The important thing is to know what this point is *before* you start negotiating. It would not be satisfactory to complete a negotiation only to discover that you won't be making any money on the deal!

By carefully considering your MUST position, you will know when a negotiation has gone outside of what you consider acceptable. You can also plan what you will do if you are unable to negotiate a satisfactory conclusion. What is your contingency plan if the negotiation collapses? In this way you establish your boundaries and you have considered the options open to you should it all go pear shaped!

I was once coaching a senior salesperson during a live negotiation where he was attempting to sign a two year deal to supply his products to a customer. He was becoming increasingly frustrated with the demands of his customer and was really struggling to cope with the seemingly endless list of things that the customer wanted in order to do a deal. The customer was threatening that unless the salesperson gave him the things he was demanding that he would sign a deal with one of the salesperson's competitors.

I asked him to make a list of the customer's demands and then attach a cost to them. I then asked him to calculate the bottom line profit that he could expect to make from the deal over the two year period. As he completed this exercise he looked shocked. If he gave the customer everything that he was demanding then he would make a huge loss!

"So what options have you got?" I asked him. He deliberated for a few moments and then said that if the only way he could secure the deal was to meet all of the customer's demands, then he was going to walk away from the business – it wasn't worth having! It looked as if the weight of the world had lifted off his shoulders. He didn't have to do the deal! In fact, he shouldn't do the deal unless it was going to be profitable for both parties.

We then spent some more time analysing the negotiation. It was unlikely that any supplier could have met the customer's initial demands and made a profit. This meant that the customer was being unrealistic and we devised a negotiation strategy that involved communicating this to the customer and proposing a more realistic and viable approach. I am pleased to say that the salesperson was successful in securing the two year contract. During the negotiation the customer started to back track considerably from his opening list of demands and appeared concerned that the salesperson was thinking of walking away. The customer needed a supplier and the supplier needed a customer! They both needed a win/win.

Knowing his walk away point put him in a stronger position. He knew what he had to do to get a workable deal and was prepared to walk away if this couldn't be achieved.

A word of caution – be very careful about bluffing where walk away points are concerned. If the other party sees you concede on something you have described as a walk away point then you are encouraging them to ignore you if you subsequently state that you are close to (or have reached) your walk away point!

There is no point in winning if be doing so you are, in fact, losing. The term "Pyrrhic Victory" is named after a Greek king Pyrrhus who suffered heavy losses in defeating the Romans in 279 BC. After people complimented him on his victory he said, "Another such victory over the Romans and we are undone."

In negotiation there is no point in securing deals and agreements that are in fact damaging. Secure too many such deals and you too could be "undone"!

I should make you aware at this stage about a dirty tactic used in a negotiation, where you are one of several people competing to secure the business. Once you have gone beyond your personal walk away point, you can carry on negotiating sharper and sharper deals before pulling out of the process and leaving the "winning" people with a deal on which they will lose money.

This is done in an attempt to weaken a competitor's business. This is a very underhand tactic and can obviously backfire very spectacularly. I am not recommending it to you; I am merely making you aware of it so you can defend yourself against it!

Planning Stage 6: Negotiation Style

The final stage of your negotiation planning is to think about the overall style and approach you are going to take during the negotiation. This step draws elements from any of the steps so far, including what your objectives are, the power balance and the personality styles involved to name but a few.

For example, a negotiation to secure a long term partnership where both parties' organisations are going to need to work very closely together over a long period of time, is likely to have a different style to a "one off" negotiation to purchase new office furniture.

Conversely, if you have a challenging and tough objective to achieve you may need to adopt a tough style. This does not mean that you are still not pursuing a "win/win" outcome.

A common misconception is that "win/win" negotiation is in some way nicer and softer than "win/lose" negotiation. Nothing could be further from the truth! Achieving a robust "win/win" negotiation can be far tougher and more challenging than simply shafting someone!

So consider what you want to achieve, the people involved, the balance of power and then decide what style is the most appropriate? To return to my double glazing example, the style I chose to adopt was based on having considered that there were a large number of potential providers available. Therefore, I could adopt a harder approach than if there was only one provider. I did not need (or want) any form of longer term relationship with the company involved, I only needed to be confident that they would still be in business to be able to honour their ten year guarantee.

Therefore, I decided to behave like a normal customer during the presentation until we arrived at the subject of price. Each double glazing salesman followed pretty much the same approach. After telling me that the double glazing would cost an exorbitant sum, they would then proceed to tell me that if we would agree to be a show home, give a testimonial, have our photo taken in front of our house holding a giant discount cheque blah, blah, blah – that they could offer a discount.

So to deliberately unsettle the salesperson (immediately after he had mentioned the first inflated price and the subsequent "special offer price") I changed personality, told him that it was all very interesting, informed him that I trained people to sell and negotiate for a living, gave him some feedback on his sales call to date (where he had done well and areas for improvement!) and asked him to "stop fu**ing about" and cut to the chase!

My plan backfired with one salesperson who was so shocked at my sudden change of behaviour that he packed his bags and left! However, with the salespeople who chose to stay, I had tipped the power balance in my favour, disturbed their normal selling process and by unsettling them had effectively got them onto their back foot.

Now you may be thinking that this does not sound like someone who preaches a "win/win" approach to negotiation. The "win/win" philosophy is my primary approach to negotiating, however I can adapt and flex my style as required and so should you.

I offer this example to demonstrate the importance of planning and then following a particular style. The double glazing companies with whom I interacted had chosen to adopt a particular approach which I anticipated and planned for.

This would be an entirely unsuitable approach to follow when I am negotiating with a potential partner for a joint venture opportunity. I love doing joint ventures with the right people and in order for these to work effectively, I choose to adopt a rigorous "win/win" approach. For a joint venture to work it has to be to the benefit of both parties. If someone joint ventures with me then I want them to be hugely motivated to make it work successfully. I carefully consider and adopt the appropriate style depending upon the individual and the circumstances. I hope you will do so too!

Negotiation Step 2: Discussing and /or Arguing

"Seek first to understand and then be understood."

Stephen R Covey

This is the first stage of the negotiation where you are face to face with the other party. Negotiations can often begin with an air of tension. Sometimes this is created by an almost unconscious perception that the negotiation will be combative.

Some negotiations can be the result of a problem or dispute between the two parties. In these cases you will be expecting tension! High levels of emotion are not uncommon in negotiation and they need to be handled sensitively.

An air of tension can also be created by unknown factors. For example, you may never have met the people you will be negotiating with before, and this can add to the feelings of uncertainty.

For these reasons this step of the negotiation process is called "discussing and/or arguing". While we may hope that communication between the people involved will be a discussion rather then an argument, in many cases an argument (at least initially) it will be!

I sometimes describe this stage as the "storm before the calm". With some negotiation situations, it seems that only after some heated discussion (people may need to express their frustrations and "get things off their chest") that progress can be made.

You can reduce the tension by remembering that your key focus at this stage of the negotiation process is to find out what the other party wants, and to communicate what you want.

Up until now your beliefs about what the other party may want are based largely upon educated guess work. You cannot be certain you are correct in your assumptions. It is important to test and clarify your understanding.

Your aim is to collect as much information as possible to enable you to make a proposal that will be mutually beneficial to everyone involved. To this end, during this stage of the negotiation, find out as much as you possible can about the other party's position, objectives, attitudes, commitment, interest and intentions by questioning and listening carefully. By questioning you can clarify, for example, the level of commitment they have to their position and the directions that they may be prepared to move in. It is very important that you understand ALL the issues before you respond with a proposal. Clarify your assumptions and establish what is important to the other party.

This process can account for up to 85% of the total time spent in the negotiation. It involves needs, wants, feelings, ideas and concerns being drawn out and exchanged to reach common agreement on the key areas under discussion. You have to agree what you are attempting to achieve before you can achieve it!

Some of the key things you need to achieve at this stage of the negotiation are:

- Exchange information
- Gain a full understanding of the issues involved
- Establish and confirm areas for discussion. These will form the basis of your proposal.
- Agree what is on each party's shopping list. What can be traded? What cannot be traded?
- Explore priorities. What are the key focus areas?
- Identify the gap between the two parties. "Your situation is X. My situation is Y."
- Get EVERYTHING onto the negotiating "table". Don't leave anything hidden.
- Manage the expectations of the other party. Through your communication with the other party and your responses to the information they share you can shape their expectations about what is going to be possible.

Negotiation Behaviour

How you behave during a negotiation, will affect the success of the negotiation. Depending on its nature, behaviour can slow a negotiation down or speed it up. It can provoke a counter productive reaction or a productive response. It can cause a negotiation deadlock or unlock the gates to a robust agreement.

It is very important to consider and develop your behaviour as a negotiator. You can exercise control over not only how you present yourself during the negotiation but also how you respond to the behaviour of the other party. Please note that I said "how you respond" not "how you react". There is a difference.

When I am explaining the important difference between responding and reacting, I describe reacting as something that happens almost without you thinking about it. You may react angrily to an implied threat that the other party makes. Responding is more considered. You can respond to an implied threat in a way that will best contribute to a successful outcome for you and for the other party. When you react you lose control, allowing your behaviour to be controlled by the other party. When you respond you keep control and *choose* how you behave. Responding gives you more choices, whereas reacting reduces your choices.

As negotiation is a process that involves people interacting and being affected by each other, it is important to consider what is good negotiation behaviour (that which contributes positively to achieving a robust outcome) and poor negotiation behaviour (that which impacts negatively on a robust outcome being achieved).

Good Negotiation Behaviour

The importance of tact

Due to the heightened tension and levels of emotion that often accompany this stage of a negotiation it is very important to be particularly tactful! For example, the language that you use can affect the state of the other party.

Describing what you wish to achieve tactfully can add positively to the negotiation process. For example:

- "I hope that at the end of this meeting we will have agreed..."

- "My aim during this meeting is to see if we can agree..."

- "I do appreciate that these are challenging issues and we want to look at any constructive proposals that can help to resolve them."

You can see how these examples help to position my intentions in a tactful and constructive manner.

Doing more listening and less talking

If you do not listen properly in a negotiation then you will miss out on all sorts of useful information that you can use to bring the negotiation to a satisfactory conclusion. In addition, not listening can cause the other party to become irritated and potentially aggressive. As you must understand what both parties need to be able to negotiate a robust agreement, you have to listen very carefully.

The subject of how to listen effectively is covered in depth in the companion volume to this book – "Bare Knuckle Selling". The oft quoted phrase, "We have two ears and one mouth – use them in that proportion" provides very good guidance for effective negotiation practice.

The use of questions

Exceptional negotiators will ask far more questions than poor negotiators. Questions serve a number of purposes in a negotiation. They can be used to gather information about the other party's position, objectives, attitudes, commitment, interest, intentions, thoughts, feelings etc. They can help you to understand where the other party is.

In addition, when you are asking the questions you tend to exercise more control over the negotiation. You are, if you like, in the driving seat. When you ask a question, people have no choice but to answer it. They may choose not to answer it out loud, but they have to process it. This fact is utilised by salespeople, negotiators, hypnotists and coaches. Questions can be highly influential as they shape people's thinking. By the skilful use of questions you can shape and direct the negotiation.

Questions can also be used to buy some thinking time. If the other party makes a proposal then asking a question about it can buy you a few moments to consider it and choose the most appropriate way to respond. It keeps them busy answering the question while you take a few moments to think!

If you disagree with something that the other party says, asking them a question about it can be a more effective way to respond than openly disagreeing with it. For example, if they were to say:

"We think £10,000 is an acceptable contribution towards the advertising costs."

You could say, "£10,000! You are joking aren't you?" or you could say, "Could you explain how you arrived at that figure?" The first reaction, while perhaps helping to manage their expectations (we will explore the best way to respond to proposals later), is likely to provoke an equally heated reaction. The second response, will get you information on how the other party has calculated the figure they are seeking. For example, the figure of £10,000 could be a well considered amount that they really need to secure, or it could be an "off the cuff" figure that they have thrown in without much thought. Either way you have gained additional information that you can use.

The four types of question

We can usefully think about four types of questions to use during negotiation. These are:

- Closed
- Open
- Probing
- Summarising

These can be remembered by way of the handy mnemonic C.O.P.S.

Closed Questions

These are used to obtain a specific answer and to check facts. Examples would include:

"Is that important to you?"

"Does anyone else need to approve this?"

Closed questions usually result in a "yes" or "no" answer.

Open Questions

These are broad, diagnostic questions that encourage the other party to talk about their situation. Open questions usually start with words such as what, when, why, how, where, who, which and usually result in a multi-word or sentence answer.

Examples would include:

"What do you want to change about your current situation?"

"You have mentioned you have some concerns. What are they?"

It is important to stress that open questions usually result in a multi-word/sentence answer and closed questions usually result in a single word answer. However, in some cases you can get a "yes" or "no" to a good open question and a long reply to a closed question!

Open questions are used to gather information, and closed questions are used to clarify what you discover and to get specific answers and commitments.

Probing Questions

These are used to explore a point the other party has made. They allow you to drill further into what has been said so that you can understand it in more detail.

Examples include:

"What makes you say that?"

"In what way do you think...?"

"How do you mean?"

"Why did you bring that up?"

A useful probing technique is to use "echo questions". An echo questions is where you use the last word or few words of what the other party says as a probing question.

An example:

"We need a significant investment."

"Significant investment?"

In this example, you are probing further to discover how the other party defines "significant investment". If you did not probe, you could make some incorrect assumptions about what "significant" means.

Summarising Questions

These are used to sum up the negotiation and to confirm the discussion you have had so far. This helps to keep the negotiation on track and to check/clarify understanding.

Examples include:

"So if I understand correctly, what you are saying is...?"

"So have we agreed that...?"

Effective negotiators summarise frequently. A good summary can ensure that your views have been understood correctly. A summary allows you to clarify that your understanding is the same as the other party's. This can avoid misunderstanding later!

Clarifying understanding

Good negotiators will make sure that their understanding is the same as the other party. During a negotiation it is good practice to frequently check that you properly understand the other party's needs, wants, demands, concessions, opinions, definitions and so forth. Don't assume you understand – check.

Testing your assumptions

It is good practice to check that the assumptions you have made (and you are likely to have needed to make some as part of your planning and preparation) are accurate. Again, like clarifying understanding – test your assumptions. Making wrong assumptions and negotiating according to those assumptions can reduce the likelihood of reaching agreement. For example, if you wrongly assume that price is the other party's primary concern and it is in fact service levels, then you may find yourself making price concessions that you didn't need to.

Being open and honest

Sometimes when I discuss this concept with people they balk at being open and honest during negotiations. They feel more comfortable playing their cards close to their chest. The problem with this approach is that this may result in the flow of information between the people involved in the negotiation being poor. To negotiate a win/win deal you need to understand the other party. It is difficult to do this when both of you aren't revealing very much. It is a point worth considering.

When I recommend being open and honest I am not advocating that you tell the other party everything, or that you give away all of your power by informing them that you are incredibly desperate to gain their business and will do anything to secure it! What I am saying is that for negotiations to succeed there has to be communication flow and being as realistically open and honest as is prudent will assist this flow.

Encouraging two way conversation

Good negotiators will ensure that there is a balance to the negotiation discussion, and will ensure that both parties get sufficient air time. Attempting to dominate available air time in a misguided attempt to gain the upper hand can, in fact, be counter-productive as you will fail to understand what is important to the other party. This behaviour can also irritate the other party.

Listen for signals

Every negotiation potentially has two solutions. The solution that meets your needs (your LIKE position), and the solution that meets the other party's needs (their LIKE position). Somewhere between these two solutions is where the actual negotiated solution will be reached. This is usually very different from either party's LIKE position.

Therefore, good negotiators will continually look out for signs or signals from the other party that they may be prepared to consider some form of movement or concession.

Sometimes these will be quite obvious and sometimes they can be quite subtle, hence the reason you need to listen and watch very carefully.

For example, the other party might say, "Our normal price is X." This could be a signal that although the normal price is X, under certain circumstances, the possibility of a different price exists. Or the other party might say, "It would be incredibly difficult for us to accept an agreement of less than five years in duration." Note that it is "incredibly difficult," but not impossible for them to agree to an agreement that covered a shorter time period.

Signals can be used to communicate to the other party that while you don't like the way that the current proposal is structured, you are willing to negotiate some changes. You are not dismissing the proposal entirely, just the way it is currently structured.

We will return to the importance of signals and how to respond to them in the next chapter.

Poor Negotiation Behaviour

Point scoring

In a negotiation, egos are involved and a common mistake that is made is for people to confuse being right, or "scoring points" with getting what they want from a negotiation. If you manage to force the other party to agree that you are right on something you might feel you have "won", however you may very well have just succeeded in annoying the other party. If the other party is wrong about something (and this is often just a matter of opinion) be graceful about it. You aren't playing a board game. The person who scores the most points in the negotiation doesn't win – in fact they might end up losing! In a negotiation the person who concludes the discussion with a robust agreement that will work has won. This usually involves the other party winning as well. Save scoring points for your next game of darts and focus on understanding what the other party wants to achieve.

Sarcasm

Somewhere close to the top of the list of behaviours that are guaranteed to piss people off in a negotiation is being sarcastic. For example, perhaps someone informs you that they may be able to offer you a 1% discount for a bulk order. You respond in a sarcastic tone of voice, "Wowee – here comes the last of the big spenders. Are you sure you can afford it?" and effectively punish them for indicating their willingness to move. By recognising their indication to offer discount you may be able to obtain some more discount. By punishing their behaviour you are reducing the likelihood of them repeating it. "Thank you for your proposal. If you were able to make that discount 6%, then we may be able to consider our order quantity," would be a better alternative.

Interrupting

When people are talking in a negotiation (particularly if they are responding to a question that you have asked them) then SHUT UP and listen to them. If you keep your mouth shut and your eyes and ears open then you will learn a lot – and the more you learn the more you earn. You will recall the two ears and one mouth ratio mentioned earlier.

On top of missing out on useful information, interrupting people annoys them and unless you are deliberately trying to annoy them as part of your negotiation strategy (which can have unexpected consequences) then don't do it.

Talking too much

At the risk of repeating myself – two ears and one mouth! In addition to the points already made, you need to be very careful about what you reveal in a negotiation and when. The more you talk the more you increase the chance that you will say something stupid!

Consider what you say and when you say it carefully.

Not listening

I do not apologise for continually stressing the importance of listening. If you are busy making too many notes, or thinking about what to say next then you can sometimes stop listening fully and miss something. Keep your focus on the other person.

Ignoring signals

As with the point made about sarcasm above, don't ignore a signal from the other party. Recognise it, respond to it and encourage the other party to expand upon it.

Blaming

Finger pointing or blaming the other party may make you feel better (usually at the expense of the other party) but it doesn't contribute anything towards a successful conclusion of your negotiation. Focus on getting the agreement not apportioning blame.

Threats

You need to be very careful about issuing threats in a negotiation. If they are not positioned very carefully they can stimulate negative behaviour. Rather like two school boys squabbling with each other in the play ground, where their pushing backwards and forwards degenerates into a fight, issuing threats can result in the same being fired back at you. This sort of behaviour can spiral downwards towards conflict very, very quickly. If you are fighting then you aren't negotiating.

Personal insults

I have experienced "professional" buyers do this to me. I have had them insult my ability, intelligence, proposals, professionalism and even my appearance. As you can tell from the front cover of this book I am actually rather a handsome sort of chap (if I keep saying it often enough someone will eventually believe me) or at the very least I'd hope to come second after Quasimodo (the hunch back of Notre Dame) in a "Who's the ugliest bloke in Europe?" competition.

Some people make personal insults to unsettle the other person and impose their power upon them. If this is done to you, recognise it for what it is, smile and ignore it.

Reacting to provocation

As mentioned above, responding to any form of provocation usually only encourages more of it. If people get a reaction then they will continue. What undermines this approach is not reacting to the provocation! Respond don't react.

I am reminded about a story I read about Buddha. According to the story when Buddha's fame began to spread it was not uncommon for people to attempt to provoke him. One time a man was shouting obscenities at Buddha, calling him all sorts of unmentionable names.

After a while Buddha asked the man, "Can I ask you a question?" The surprised man said that Buddha could. Buddha asked, "If you were to offer me a gift and I refused to accept it, who would the gift belong to?" The man replied angrily, "To me – obviously!" At which Buddha smiled and walked on his way. I think Buddha would have been an interesting individual to negotiate with – he certainly understood the power of asking questions!

Becoming emotional

While it is good negotiation practice to share how you are feeling with the other party, this is very different from actually demonstrating the emotion. Saying, "I am frustrated that we have not been able to agree upon this point. Can you explain your reluctance to move on this area?" would be likely to make a positive contribution to a negotiation. Whereas, "Look for f***ks sake, this is fu**ing ridiculous, I've had enough of this crap, either you move on this or you can stick this deal up your arse!" is probably not going to contribute particularly positively to agreeing a good outcome.

As frustrating as negotiations get sometimes get, keep your cool, keep asking questions, and exploring ways to get what both parties want. Losing your cool can make you appear unprofessional and is a weakness that many negotiators will exploit to their advantage.

In the next chapter we will take a closer look at signals and then look at how to make effective proposals. I'll see you over the page!

Negotiation Step 3: Signals & Proposals

As mentioned in the last chapter, negotiations potentially have two solutions – the solution that gives you everything you want, and the solution that meets what the other party wants.

It goes without saying that it is very rare for negotiations to be successfully concluded at either of these extremes. This would require one party totally accepting the other party's demands. A more common situation is for the agreement to be concluded somewhere between each party's ideal outcome.

Therefore, as a good negotiator, you need to be always looking and listening for signs or signals from the other party that they may be prepared to consider some movement or concession.

In the same way you can use signals to communicate to the other party that even though you don't like the structure of their current proposal, you are willing to consider it favourably if some changes are made. You are not dismissing the proposal entirely, just the way it is currently presented.

Although I have used the concept of each party having an ideal outcome and the negotiation concluding somewhere in between these, please do not allow this to limit your thinking. A powerful reason to respond effectively to signals and proposals is that these may contain the possibility for negotiating an agreement that is far superior to anything either party could have considered prior to the negotiation commencing.

By exploring synergies between you, creative solutions can be generated that deliver benefits far in excess of your initial ideal outcomes. This sort of synergistic solution is usually only possible where both parties adopt a win/win mind set and approach. This is another benefit to the win/win approach.

A signal is a sign to the other party that agreement could be possible if they make some alterations and amendments to their proposal. You are inviting the other party to make a move.

If you don't send out any invitations for your birthday party then nobody is going to turn up. In the same way if you don't respond effectively to signals then you can't send any invitations to the other party.

Respond Effectively To Signals

During a negotiation when someone makes a signal it is vitally important to respond effectively. If you miss it or ignore it, it may not be made again and you will have missed an important opportunity to create the agreement you are looking for.

So, respond effectively by listening, summarising what the other person has said to make sure you understand it correctly and to give you time to consider your response, and then encourage them to expand further. For example:

"Under what circumstances would you be able to alter the specification?"

"How could I make it easier for you to agree to the proposed fee?"

If handled correctly signals are the bridge to proposals and proposals help to advance a negotiation to a satisfactory conclusion. We shall explore this a little later in this chapter.

Sending Signals Yourself

As well as remaining observant for signals from the other party you may very well want to send a signal yourself. This needs to be done correctly to ensure they are not perceived as the first signs of your willingness to make huge concessions or wave the white flag of surrender!

Therefore, it is important to structure your signal so that the hint of movement on your part is conditional on the other party responding positively. You are not giving away the family silver for no return! You imply a willingness to negotiate, but only if the other party reciprocates. You need to attach a qualification to your statement. In the examples quoted earlier we considered the example:

"It would be incredibly difficult for us to accept an agreement of less than five years in duration." This signals the possibility of movement. You are indicating that there is the possibility of flexibility. You are not saying that you will agree to an agreement of less than five years – you are signalling that you are prepared to discuss it. The use of the word "difficult" implies that the other party will need to provide some incentive for you to make some movement. You are indicating that although the current proposal is unacceptable, you are willing to negotiate. You are inviting the other party to move forwards in the negotiation. Signals, if handled correctly, move the negotiation forward. Signals often result in proposals.

Proposals

When proposals are made they tend to contribute positively to the negotiation moving forward. Making a proposal is far better than continuing to argue! While it is far better to wait for the other party to make their proposal first (as this then gives you information that you can respond to) do not be afraid to make proposals yourself. A proposal is far better than a deadlock. And as stated previously, if nobody plays a card then there is no game to be played!

You will be in a position to make a proposal when you are able to accurately summarise what the other party wants to achieve. You should also make sure that, prior to making your proposal, the other party understands what you want to achieve. When this has been achieved, the ground has been set for proposals to be made.

When making a proposal yourself the common wisdom is to "pad" your proposal. That is if you want to sell a property for £500,000 then you would "pad" your opening price proposal at say, £550,000 to allow yourself some negotiating room. Obviously, the other party will also know how the game is being played and will be expecting you to "pad" your proposal.

Although this might seem like ridiculous nonsense (if everyone knows what is going on, then why don't we just cut to the chase?) it is very common practice and you will therefore need to consider how you approach this.

To begin with it is good negotiation practice to never accept someone's first offer. Most people will "pad" their initial price. When I was on honeymoon with my wife (I'm hardly likely to be on honeymoon with anyone else am I?) we came across a guy offering horse and carriage sightseeing tours. He beckoned us over and asked us if we would like a forty-five minute horse drawn sightseeing tour. Karen said that she would like to do it and, particularly as we were on honeymoon, it seemed like a nice idea. I'm such a romantic!

"How much?" I asked. The guy told me, and the equivalent cost in sterling was about £5. "Excellent!" I said and jumped on board. The guy looked visibly shocked, like he couldn't believe his luck and was still looking somewhat shell-shocked when I handed him the money at the end of an excellent sightseeing tour.

What can we learn from this? Well firstly, he wasn't expecting to get £5. He was expecting me to haggle. He was maybe expecting to get £2, £3 or maybe £4. So was he happy with his £5. Yes and no. Yes, as Simon "last of the big spenders" Hazeldine has agreed to his quoted price without question. No, because as he was taking us on our sightseeing trip he was probably wondering how much more he could have asked for and got. While £5 may have been worth more to him than me, I would have quite happily paid more. I'm on my honeymoon for chrissakes!

He may have spent the forty-five minutes gently fuming at his missed opportunity.

And what about me? Well as it was only a fiver I didn't really give it much thought. The sightseeing tour sounded really nice, Karen wanted to do it, we were on honeymoon, so let's go! No big deal. But as we were relaxing on our sightseeing tour I did say to Karen, "I should have haggled, I could have got this cheaper!" But it was only a few measly pounds right? Big deal!

Yes – big deal! Take this concept and apply it to a negotiation involving a higher ticket. Imagine negotiating with me over a £500,000 contract. You ask me how much I am going to charge to provide my consultancy services to you for a year.

I say, "£500,000". You say "Okay." What a deal! However afterwards I am going to be thinking, "I should have asked for £600,000 – this person must be loaded!" and you might be thinking "I shouldn't have agreed to pay that – I bet Hazeldine's padded his price."

Neither of us is very satisfied! So never accept the first offer – for the sake of both parties!

Having learned my lesson on honeymoon (at a cost of the £2 or £3 - a pretty cheap lesson in negotiation – if you want to attend one of my negotiation training bootcamps it is going to cost you rather more than that!) I now never accept anyone's first offer.

So, good practice when making a proposal is to get the balance right. Open realistically. A realistic proposal will be credible and be aimed at your LIKE position and the other party's MUST position. Too much padding will cause problems later (as we will see in a moment), however it is a common failing of negotiators to err too far on the side of caution, aiming lower when they should be aiming higher.

To illustrate the danger of excessive padding, I mentioned earlier that I was recently purchasing double glazing for my new house. One of the salespeople went through the usual routine, measured all of the windows and doors and worked out a price.

I sat with Karen on the settee in our lounge waiting for him to make a price proposal so that the fun could really begin. He finished tapping numbers into his calculator and then announced:

"Mr and Mrs Hazeldine, I have been doing some calculations to ensure you get the very best price. As you are having all of your windows and doors double glazed I can do it for £24,000."

I was just about to adopt my very best "You are joking pal!" face when he instantly followed up by saying, "However, you've got a lovely house and if you agree to be one of our exclusive show homes in this area and you sign up tonight I can do it for £12,000."

In a matter of a few seconds he had halved his price. How credible is that? Not very! He has made a few mistakes. Firstly, he has used nice round numbers like £12,000. Good negotiators don't use big round numbers as they are just begging to be negotiated! Secondly, he has just cut his price in half on the spot. I am now wondering if he has cut his price in half once I wonder if he can do it again? And thirdly, he has no idea what I do for a living, although he is about to find out very soon...

To cut a long story short we ended up agreeing to pay £6,300 for the double glazing (almost half again) and a somewhat dishevelled salesperson left us after a hard evenings work! The double glazing company agreed to a fitting date with us and then two days before they were due to fit our windows phoned to re-arrange the fitting date because they were short staffed. We weren't in any rush to have the windows fitted but I took the opportunity to negotiate the price down by a further £500 for our "inconvenience". So we ended up paying £5800 (I knew I could half the £12,000) to have all of our windows and doors double glazed.

I should also mention that this was not the lowest price we were quoted. I did secure a price of £4400 from one company but due to the lack of professionalism of their salespeople I began to doubt that they would do a good job and chose to pay more to another company who were more reputable. My aim was not to get double glazing fitted at the cheapest price. My aim was to get good quality double glazing fitted at the best possible price. It is never just about price!

Open credibly and realistically, it provides a solid foundation to negotiate from. A ridiculous opening position that you retreat from rapidly makes you look like an amateur and you run the risk of being taken to the cleaners!

The "Magic Negotiation Formula" – Conditional Proposals

I'd really like you to pay close attention to this section. The reason I say that is because the tactic that I am going to reveal to you is one of the most important things you will ever learn about negotiation. When I learned this simple formula my negotiations were transformed! And it is so, so simple.

The secret is that when you make proposals in a negotiation you make them *conditional*. This means that the other party can only gain from your proposal if they agree to the conditions that are attached to it. They will only benefit if they agree to the terms of your proposal. The proposal has two elements:

1. The condition
2. The offer

The structure that you use to communicate your conditional proposal is very important. This is known as the "If you...Then I..."

formula. You state the condition first and the offer second. For example:

"If you agree to grant us exclusive rights for the United Kingdom then we will re-think our promotional calendar for the forthcoming year."

The structure is:

"IF YOU *agree to grant us exclusive rights for the United Kingdom* (the condition) THEN WE *will re-think our promotional calendar for the forthcoming year* (the offer)."

In addition you will notice that the condition (If you agree to grant us exclusive rights for the United Kingdom) is specific and the offer (we will re-think our promotional calendar for the forthcoming year) is somewhat vague!

Your conditions do not always have to be as specific, they can be vague if required. However your proposal must be vague. The reason for this is that until you know if your proposal is acceptable then it is important to give yourself some flexibility and room for movement. A vague proposal allows you to negotiate and make some movement without being seen to "give in".

You can use the following phrases to make your proposals suitably vague e.g.

"I will re-think..."

"We will consider..."

"I can look at..."

"I can re-think..."

"We can explore..."

This formula is very powerful so please make it a habit when you are negotiating.

It ensures that the other party can only benefit if they agree to your proposal. Consider the impact of getting the formula wrong and of not making your proposal suitably vague:

"We will give your product lead feature every month in our promotional calendar for the next year if you give us exclusive rights for the United Kingdom."

Can you see how much weaker this is? In this example, not only does the negotiator make a very specific proposal that ties up his promotional calendar for the next year but he has offered this before he knows that the other party has any interest in his proposal. In addition, when the proposal is made before the condition, it encourages the other party to take the benefit of the proposal without giving anything in return!

In negotiation we give to get. We don't just give!

Once you have made your conditional proposal, you may need to explain it further. When this has been done, it is a good idea to summarise and then invite the other party to respond to your proposal. Then listen carefully to what they say and proceed with the negotiation.

How To Receive A Proposal From The Other Party

As well as making proposals you will also be on the receiving end of them. It is important to receive them correctly. Listen carefully and do not interrupt the other party. When they have made their proposal think about why they have made it? What has motivated them? What are the needs that have prompted this proposal? Can you help them to get what they are looking for in a way that will benefit you?

There are a number of ways that you can respond to a proposal once it has been made and you have thought about what lies behind it. You can:

1. Say "No". This will leave the other party with the initiative and will often not contribute very positively to the negotiation.

2. Say "Yes". If the proposal meets your needs then you may very well wish to agree. However, before you do – is this an opportunity to secure something else from your shopping list?

3. Adjourn to consider. If the proposal is of interest but you need more time to think about it then you can always ask to adjourn the negotiation for as long as is required. Major negotiations will often consist of a series of adjournments.

4. Make a counter proposal. Using the conditional proposal structure you may choose to respond with your own proposal. This is usually the best way to respond to a proposal. What do you need to have to be able to agree to their proposal? Can you give them what they want but in a way that suits you? This approach will often result in you getting what you want and the other party getting what they want.

Don't dismiss proposals before you have explored how you can make them acceptable to both parties. A good way to do this is to ask open questions and encourage the other party to expand upon their proposal and make it more attractive to you. Keep exploring – how you can give them what they want and make sure you get what you want? Don't dismiss proposals – use them as springboards to make your own counter proposals.

As you can see proposals are leading into the exciting stage of the negotiation known as bargaining. Please join me in the next chapter where you will learn how to bargain profitably.

Negotiation Step 4: Bargain

This is often an exciting stage of the negotiation process as the possibility of a successful outcome is in sight. Because of this, it is vitally important that you don't allow yourself to get carried away when you scent potential victory! If this happens, in your haste to close the deal, you may make concessions that end up proving costly.

For negotiations to succeed there will usually have to be some trading; some movement and concessions being made. You will trade variable elements with the other party so that you can both achieve items on your respective shopping lists. It is important to remember that in negotiations you give to get. You do not just give! You must bargain profitably.

The following guidelines should be followed:

Use The "If You...Then I" Conditional Proposal Structure

As discussed in the last chapter, when making proposals, always make sure that the other party can only benefit from your offer if they agree to the conditions attached to it. As proposals will often lead to counter proposals and then to further counter proposals, continue to use the "If You...Then I" conditional proposal structure.

Stick To Your Pre–prepared List of Variable Factors

There is little point in planning and preparing if you deviate from it! While I am a strong advocate of creativity and flexibility during negotiation, you need to be very careful about making any concessions that you have not carefully thought through. What seems like a good idea in the moment may turn out to be very costly when fully considered.

Just Clear The Hurdles

If you watch athletes competing in a hurdle race you will notice that they only just clear the hurdles – they know that to jump higher than required to clear the hurdle is inefficient and may cost them the race. Indeed you will often see hurdles being knocked over as the athletes aim to clear the hurdle by the slightest margin and in their quest for efficiency actually hit the hurdle.

When trading variables you need to clear the required hurdle by the slightest margin possible. You need to only just get over the requirements of the other party or indeed hit it exactly. If they need 30 days credit to make the deal work then you need to give them 30 days or less. You don't give them 40 or 50 days. If they need a deposit of £4,300 to secure the deal then you give them £4,300 not £5,000. Make it tough! Trade grudgingly and make the other party work hard to get your concessions.

In negotiations you need to be careful of the signals you are sending. Conceding too quickly or conceding too generously may send the signal that you are overly keen to secure the deal and that you have more to offer! An experienced negotiator will pick up signals like a shark scents blood in the water. If they sense that there is more to be had then they will pursue you like a ravenous Great White!

Make Your Concessions Smaller and Smaller

As the agreement moves closer and closer to a conclusion, make your concessions smaller and smaller. This sends the signal that you have very little, if anything, left to concede. Using money as an example, a decreasing discount concession (remembering, of course, to gain something of equal or greater value in return for each concession) could be:

Concession 1: £97

Concession 2: £10

Concession 3: £3

Concession 4 : 7p

This is, of course, a very artificial example. However, it illustrates that each time a concession is made it is smaller and smaller. This sends a clear message to the other party that you are only able to make smaller and smaller concessions.

Contrast this with the signal you send if the concessions increase in price each time they are made:

Concession 1: £5

Concession 2: £67

Concession 3: £158

Concession 4 : £1,234

If you were getting concessions that increased each time they were granted then this would encourage you (you Great White Shark you!) that there was lots more to be gained! This deal just keeps getting richer and richer! You would be thinking, "If I keep on pushing and asking I am going to get such a good deal!" The signals that are being sent are that the concessions get bigger the more you ask. So what do you do? You keep asking, of course!

Watch Out For The Round Numbers

The figures people use in negotiations are important. As mentioned previously the double glazing salesman I was negotiating with used round numbers like £24,000 and £12,000, and these are crying out to be negotiated.

A figure such as £6,743 is more credible (providing that you can explain and justify it if challenged) than a round number such as £6,500. I always pursue round numbers with vigour! If I invest an hour into reducing a price from say £7,000 to £6,543 then I have saved £457. You could view this as earning £457. And earning £457 for an hour's work is pretty good wages for many people.

Trade Oxo Cubes For Tea Chests

If you were to put an Oxo Cube and a tea chest (the sort that people used to pack their possessions in when moving house) on the floor alongside each other, then the tea chest would dwarf the Oxo Cube. This concept is used to illustrate that you should:

1. Trade items that are low cost (Oxo Cube) to you but high value (Tea Chest) to the other party

2. Emphasise the value of your variables and devalue the value of the other party's variables

For example, when buying property you could be flexible upon when you sign a contract. You could be in a position to sign immediately or delay a month or so. Depending upon the other party's position they might really need an instant sale or they might need to wait. Let us assume that you can proceed whenever you want and the other party has a specific date by which they must have the sale finalised by.

It doesn't make a lot of difference to you when the deal is closed. It does matter enormously to the other party though and you can use this to leverage some concessions that you want. You can only do this if you communicate that if the other party agree to give you some, or all, of the things that you want then you may be in a position to be somewhat flexible on timing. You need to emphasise the value of your concession (e.g. how difficult it is for you to wait a month, how you have other properties to consider, how you really need to sign the contract as soon as possible as you need to transfer the money before the end of the month etc.) so that you can leverage some concessions from the other party that you want e.g. free decorating, free building work, free furniture, a discounted price etc.

You will find it easier to gain concessions from the other party that are low cost to them. For example, someone could have a customer email list of 100,000 customers who have bought a book on property development. It costs almost nothing for them to email this list of customers recommending a seminar on property development. If you were running a seminar on property development that cost each person attending £500 and just 0.25% of the people emailed signed up then you would make £125,000 in ticket sales!

Although it would cost very little to email the list if you owned it, you would emphasise during the negotiation the value of it, that you rarely (if ever) emailed other people's offers to it, that you had never endorsed a seminar before etc. etc.

Look for concessions that cost the other party little but are high value for you. And even if a concession is low cost to you, emphasise the value of it to the other party so you can leverage things you want in return.

Never give without getting. Give nothing away for free. Communicate strongly to the other party that you will concede nothing unless this is matched by a similar effort on their part.

Don't Get Picked Off

You need to keep the "big picture" of the overall agreement in sight at all times. Don't allow the other party to cherry pick concessions or to pick off separate little agreements during the negotiation. It is OK to agree in principle to various elements of the deal but stress that *nothing* is agreed until *everything* is agreed. Make sure that all the elements are linked together to prevent the other party treating the negotiation as a pick and mix sweet counter and only selecting the things they want.

Be Unreasonable

If the other party makes an unreasonable demand don't say no. Instead respond with an equally unreasonable request for a concession in return! I was once negotiating with a major retail chain on behalf of a world famous branded product. The brand was currently sponsoring a film season on television. I had been asked to negotiate a major promotional feature in the retail estate that featured the television sponsorship. The buyer I was negotiating with asked if I could arrange for his company to be featured as a co-sponsor on television. He was, in effect, asking for hundreds of thousands of pounds of television exposure for free!

I didn't say no. I said that to make it financially worthwhile for me to give him that level of television exposure that would probably need to de-list every single competitor brand from his entire retail estate! He obviously couldn't agree to this and the negotiation progressed. However, I did agree to several advertisement features in major newspapers (in return for securing the promotional exposure and the sales increase that I wanted) instead. This story illustrates firstly how to respond to outrageous requests and secondly emphasises that if you aim for the stars (major television exposure) you can sometimes land on the moon (major newspaper exposure). If someone asks for something unreasonable ask for something unreasonable in return. And make some unreasonable requests yourself – you may get some interesting responses!

Don't Reject – Propose An Alternative

If, during the bargaining stage, the other party rejects your offer then ask them to propose an alternative. This keeps the negotiation moving and provides you with more information. In the same way, if you receive an offer that is unacceptable, don't just reject it – propose an alternative. This helps to prevent negotiations becoming deadlocked.

On the subject of deadlocks – these can occur at any stage in a negotiation. Deadlocks are when the negotiation stalls and there seems to be no way forward. Not all deadlocks are genuine. If the other party knows you have a deadline by which the negotiation must be concluded then this can be used as a pressure tactic. By appearing to hit a deadlock (one way to do this is to insist upon an unacceptable or unreasonable condition being agreed to) the other party puts pressure on you to make concessions to keep the negotiation moving so that you can hit your deadline!

To move out of genuine deadlocks (and sometimes less then genuine ones) make proposals. A good proposal can get the discussion started again, as can starting to bargain around a deadlocked proposal. Another way to get around deadlocks is to take a break from the negotiation or agree to reconvene at a later time or date. This change can often help both parties to recommence with a different mind set.

When you are close to agreement during the bargaining stage it is time once more to summarise. So let's do exactly that over the page.

Negotiation Step 5: Summarise

Although the power of summarising at any stage of the negotiation has been mentioned previously, it is particularly important at this stage of the negotiation process.

To summarise what has been discussed about summarising so far:

Summarising:

- Helps to simplify the varied, and perhaps complex, issues that may be under discussion in the negotiation

- Helps to focus the negotiation on key issues and topics

- Helps you to keep control of the negotiation - it is sometimes said that, "He who summarises the negotiation controls the negotiation"

- Shows the other party that you are listening to what they are saying

- Shows the other party that you are paying careful attention

- Can give you valuable seconds to think by summarising before you respond

When the bargaining stage is reaching a conclusion, it is time to summarise as a distinct and important stage of the negotiation.

Elements to include during this summary are:

- Summarise they key issues that have been preventing agreement so far

- Summarise your understanding of the revised or new proposal

- Use closed questions ("Is this correct?", "Do you agree with my summary?") to gain confirmation from the other party

If they say "yes" then you are close to being able to close the deal! If they say "no", then you will need to explore with them why not, and most likely re-enter the bargaining stage. From a "no" response you will have a number of options depending upon the circumstances:

1. Resolve the areas of disagreement that remain

2. Adjourn to re-consider your situation, approach, proposal etc.

3. Walk away from the deal if you cannot resolve it

Having reached this summary stage, in many cases, you will be ready to move the negotiation to a satisfactory conclusion for both parties by closing the deal.

Negotiation Step 6: Close & Agree

The deal is in sight my Bare Knuckle Negotiators! You are close to getting an agreement that is going to work for both parties.

To make this a reality you are going to have to close the deal. In the same way that closing sales is vital to sales success, closing a deal is vital to negotiation success.

Closing a negotiation is broadly similar to closing a sale. As the companion book to this title, "Bare Knuckle Selling", covers closing in considerable detail, I shall confine this chapter to exploring the key points as they apply to negotiation.

Your aim at this stage is, having got both parties to agree to a workable deal, to conclude the negotiation and move forward to actually making the deal live.

Trial Closing

Testing the water with trial closing can be a useful way of moving to a final close by ensuring that all relevant issues have been included:

"So are you saying that if I agree to this concession that you will be satisfied?"

This ensures that there is nothing else to consider, and that there are no late "surprises" from the other party.

Close On A Question

An effective closing method during negotiation is to use a relatively minor question as an opportunity to conclude the deal. For example if the other party asks if you will include the carpets and curtains with a property sale, you can say:

"If you agree to buy the property at the agreed price, then I will include the carpets and curtains."

You will notice that at this stage, as you are going for the close, that the conditional proposal is more specific than previously. If they agree to buy then you will agree to include the carpets and curtains, whereas previously you may have indicated that you would consider including the carpets and curtains. You are aiming to close at this stage and need to be more specific and pointed than at earlier stages in the negotiation.

However, be very careful when making closing concessions. If you make them, then make them conditional on acceptance of the proposal and make them very specific, and very small!

Another good way to close is just to assume the deal is done and say, "Okay, it seems as if we are both satisfied – shall we get the paperwork done?" or "We have agreement. Shall I get confirmation to you in writing?"

This is often enough to nudge the agreement forward to conclusion.

If you get a "yes", agree who is going to take what action and when. Ensure that both parties have clarity about what will happen next and then follow up the agreement in writing or with whatever legal documentation is required.

If at all possible be the party who clarifies the agreement in writing. This keeps you in a position of control and prevents any "additional interpretation" of the final agreement by the other party!

Now all you have to do is to make the deal work. And that is the subject of the next chapter!

Negotiation Step 7: Making The Agreement Live

To begin this chapter let me reiterate an important point. Verbal agreements, written agreements and even legal contracts don't make deals work – people do. Although it is sensible business practice to have a clear legal agreement when necessary (for example, I have one with my publishers for this book) don't make the mistake of thinking that once the signatures are on the contract that the deal is done.

Should the other party not fulfil their part of the bargain you can, of course, use the power of the legal agreement or contract to force them to fulfil their side of the bargain. However, this will involve expensive lawyers, solicitors and barristers (law is a very well paid profession!) and usually a long time period!

So a good negotiator will not rely on the agreement. They know that they have to make the agreement work. This means making the people involved work.

People are motivated to work when there is some reward for them. This is one of the strongest reasons that having a win/win approach is so vital. A loser has no desire or motivation to help you win! Unless there is some gain for the other party they will not be motivated to make the deal work.

I have a simple agreement with a joint venture partner to promote my "Bare Knuckle Selling" and "Bare Knuckle Negotiating" Boot Camp seminars in the UK. My joint venture partner organises and markets the seminars to his customer base in the UK and I deliver them. The deal is simple. After promotional, staging and administrative costs have been taken into account, we split the profit 50/50. He gets half and I get half. In this way we are both motivated to make the events work and we are both motivated to fulfil our part of the bargain.

Consider this for a moment. How motivated would I be to run the seminar for 10% of the profits? Certainly not as motivated as I am for 50% of the profits! And how motivated would my joint venture partner be to promote and organise the seminars for 10% of the profits? Not as motivated as he is for 50% of the profits!

In addition, due to the arrangement, we both have a vested interest in making the arrangement work. If I don't fulfil my part of the bargain, my joint venture partner loses out. If my joint venture partner doesn't fulfil his part of the bargain I lose out.

Or to put it another way – do you want someone 10% motivated to make an agreement work or 100% motivated to make a deal work? You don't have to be a mathematical genius to work out that a 50% profit margin from a partner with a strong motivation to make a deal work is worth far more than a 75% profit margin from a "partner" with little motivation to make it work. 75% of nothing is... well... nothing!

I will often say that the real work starts *after* you have got an agreement. Don't think your job as a negotiator finishes when you leave the negotiation table. Leave the negotiation table with a clear understanding and action plan of exactly how you, and the other party, are going to make the agreement work

In my book "Bare Knuckle Selling" I discuss the four types of people involved in a decision making process. These are the decision influencers, makers, owners and implementers. In large organisations (and in many smaller organisations) for a negotiated agreement to work you need to make sure that all four of these people are clear about what they have to do and are motivated to do it.

1. Decision Influencers

These are the individuals (or groups of individuals) who want to be involved or whom the decision maker wants to be involved. Usually if they say "no" that means a "no" to the decision. However, it does not follow that if they say "yes" that you will get a "yes". These people can exert a very powerful influence over the negotiation process and also need to be supportive of making the final agreement work.

2. Decision Makers

These are the individuals (or groups of individuals) who weigh all the available information and options and who make the decision and will often conduct the negotiation. Again they need to be on-side during the negotiation and during the implementation stage that follows.

3. Decision Owners

This is the individual (or individuals) who takes "ownership" of the decision and is accountable for the results. The negotiated agreement may be delegated to these individuals. They will need to make the agreement work. If you don't have these people on side then your agreement will never become a reality!

4. Decision Implementers

These are the individuals who make the "yes" decision a reality. If you like, they are the people who actually do the work! It can be a fatal mistake to not include these people in making the agreement work. Sometimes, this can be as simple as spending some time listening to their thoughts, ideas and concerns. As simple as it sounds this can be often be enough to make an agreement work. Involvement enhances motivation and this is what makes deals work.

Please note that these people may not be four distinct individuals. One person may fulfil more than one role.

Invest as much time and effort into making the deal work as you did in agreeing it in the first place and you maximise your chances of success. Far too many agreements fall apart and when the results aren't delivered you can find yourself back at the negotiating table trying to negotiate your way out of a mess! Far better to put the effort into making the agreement you have work for both parties than ending up in court for "breach of contract"!

Always remember – agreements don't work on their own. *People* make them work.

The Dark Side of Negotiation

No book on negotiating would be complete without exploring the "dark side" of negotiation. Unless you are very lucky you will certainly encounter people whose idea of successful negotiating is to flay you alive! There are people who pursue win/lose negotiating with a vengeance. They want to win and they are prepared to do pretty much anything to do so. They will cheat, lie, manipulate and intimidate you. Or at least they will if you let them.

While I will, if the situation is appropriate, choose to adopt a more win/lose, one off, transactional approach in my negotiations, my preferred approach is win/win.

With the above in mind I include the details of what follows for two reasons:

1. So that after careful consideration you can use some of these techniques. Please only do so when you have fully considered the potential repercussions. Please don't come crying to me when your win/lose agreements don't deliver or when people don't trust you anymore!

2. So that you can understand these techniques and plan and prepare for when (and I do mean when and not if) someone tries to use these against you.

I would strongly recommend that you focus on improving your overall skill as a negotiator rather than on learning a few "quick and dirty" tactics. Firstly, you will build a reputation that will make people want to do business with you, and secondly anyone who is any good is able to deal with someone using any of the techniques and tactics that follow anyway.

Having had direct experience of every thing that follows, I can tell you that understanding the tactic or technique often drains it of its power. When you understand it for what it is – a tactic – you will be able to handle it more effectively.

With this in mind let us begin our journey into the dark side of negotiation...

Power Plays

There are a number of things that people may do in order to intimidate you, or to make them seem more powerful than you are. While understanding and working with the power balance is vitally important to negotiation success, some people interpret this to mean bullying the other person into submission!

Some examples of power play behaviour are:

Unilaterally controlling the agenda

The refusal to allow the other party to have any say in the topics and areas under negotiation is an attempt by the individual to impose their will upon the other person. Accepting this will mean that the negotiation is confined to areas that only suit the aggressive party. In addition, taking control early in a negotiation can send signals about who has the power! If you accept this behaviour you are, in effect, agreeing with it. The negotiation over what will be negotiated is an important part of the negotiation!

Aggressive behaviour

Shouting, swearing, finger pointing, threats, non-verbal intimidation (standing over people, invading their body space etc.) are all designed to intimidate. Make it clear that you do not submit to intimidation, bullying or threats. Make it clear that they will only get something from you if they provide good reasons *and* give you something you want in return. You don't have to be a violent thug to be tough. Toughness comes from a firm and focused approach that does not give in to intimidation. The great man of peace Mahatma Ghandi had a reputation for being as "hard as nails", without ever resorting to any form of aggressive behaviour – and look at his track record as a negotiator!

Sudden changes of behaviour

One method of intimidation that I particularly want to highlight is a sudden change of behaviour. This works by adopting a certain mode of behaviour (discussing the topic under negotiation fairly calmly for example) and then suddenly becoming aggressive and hostile. The suddenness of this change can trigger the primitive fight/flight response and unsettle the other party. The few seconds of shock can be enough to drive home a point while the other party is off guard. I have used a milder version on occasion to interrupt another party's preferred pattern of negotiating, and then used this moment to shift the direction of a negotiation. Use this with care and only if you have fully considered its impact and possible effects and consequences. If it is used against you, understand it for what it is and regain your composure as quickly as possible.

Rubbishing you, your ideas, your products, your services

Sometimes in an attempt to tip the power balance people will rubbish or dismiss your ideas and suggestions ("That's a stupid idea"), you as an individual ("You haven't done this before have you?"), your products ("We can get cheap and tacky products like this from a hundred suppliers") or your services ("We can buy sales training from any number of people with more experience than you"). If this is done to me, I just smile to myself. If what they are saying is true, then why are they bothering to negotiate with me in the first place?

Attempting to irritate you

Using a combination of rubbishing, insults, goading, delaying and any other dirty tactic some negotiators will deliberately try to annoy and irritate you. They do this so that you are not in a balanced and resourceful state. I am sure that most of us have had the experience of saying something in anger that we later regret. That is exactly the aim of attempting to irritate the other party. If they succeed they have exercised some control over you. Do your best to avoid being drawn. Martial artists say, "Keep your mind like calm water."

Intimidating you

There are a variety of methods people use to get you onto the back foot. These include:

- The big desk/office. Some people like to communicate their power by sitting behind a desk big enough to land a small plane on, which is in an office the size of a small football pitch. This apparently communicates their power and authority!

- **Lower chair.** Along with the big office and desk often comes the low chair. The chair that you sit on is lower than their chair! This means that they look down on you. This is designed to communicate power. Although the effects can be subtle do not overlook the influence the environment can have upon your assessment of the power balance.

- **Keeping you waiting.** Waiting around for half an hour or longer means that you are summoned to the negotiation when *they* are ready for you. Again, designed to put you on the back foot. I used to have a customer who routinely kept me waiting for forty five minutes. I used to take some paper work to do and spread out across the table in his reception area. When I was finally summoned, I kept *him* waiting while I packed up all of my paper work!

- **The power handshake.** This is nothing to do with secret Masonic handshakes! This is a method of non-verbal intimidation. When going to shake someone's hand the power handshake is delivered by offering your hand with the palm facing down. To be able to shake your hand the other person has to turn their palm face up. Body language experts think that this forces the person with their palm upwards into a more submissive position. I'm not sure if this is true or not, but I have been on the receiving end of such a handshake on more than one occasion.

As mentioned earlier in the book, true power is in the mind and if you have planned and prepared correctly you will be less affected by attempts at power play. Do not make the mistake of thinking that these techniques aren't effective. Sometimes they can be very effective. The best way to inoculate your self from them is to understand them and then recognise them. This will diminish or even neutralise their effect upon you.

Dirty Tricks & Tactics

As promised here is a collection of some less savoury tricks and tactics that you may encounter when negotiating!

There are a number of tactics that make use of someone other than the person you are negotiating with to force or "encourage" you to agree to some form of concession. These are:

"Good Cop/Bad Cop"

Anyone who has watched enough police shows on television will have seen the interrogation tactic where one cop is nasty and one cop is nice. One cop shouts and threatens the suspect while the other befriends him and is nice to him. Although this tactic is widely known it can still be a very effective way to manipulate someone's behaviour.

The human system is primarily prompted to take action to either avoid pain/discomfort (away from motivation) or to gain comfort/pleasure (towards motivation). These motivating forces operate at a deep, and sometimes unconscious, level in human neurology. If you consider the "Good Cop/Bad Cop" tactic with an understanding of the deep seated towards/away from motivation then you will understand why it can be so effective. Even though we all know about this tactic (perhaps we watch too much television!) we may not understand the unconscious motivating factors that make it so effective. Some people will feel under pressure and stressed during negotiation and this combined with the towards/away from motivation can make the individual more susceptible to this sort of manipulation.

The best way to defend yourself from this tactic is to firstly understand it, secondly to become aware that despite knowing about it you may still be manipulated by it, and thirdly, you may wish to even say (perhaps in a humorous sort of way) "Hey, what is this? Good cop, bad cop?" This will help to diffuse the tension involved and make the other party aware that you have sussed their game.

"My Boss Is A Bastard!"

Another people based tactic is where the person you are negotiating with attempts to convince you that you really ought to agree to what they are asking for, as if the negotiation has to be escalated to their boss then you will be in BIG trouble.

The implication is that you will get a better deal if you agree to what *they* are asking for. If their boss gets involved then it is going to get even worse. I used to deal with a buyer who would use this frequently. He would attempt to convince me that he didn't really want to involve his boss, as he was a real hard taskmaster. In addition the implication was that he was trying to help me and that I ought to be grateful for his assistance!

The counter to this is to firstly, inform the other person that you too have a real bastard of a boss (if you don't have a boss then you may wish to use another person – a business partner perhaps) and secondly, to be fully prepared to negotiate with the boss. This can be even better for you as the boss will have a higher authority level within the organisation! Very often people will not want their boss involved as it will look as if they cannot do their job properly and they are only mentioning their boss to get you to give them what they want.

"I Need To Get This Approved By My Boss"

During a negotiation this tactic is utilised to get you to make your proposals and concessions concrete and the return from the other party less so! You will be asked to confirm your proposal and in return the other party will tell you that they "would love to confirm back to you but that they need to get it approved by their boss". You are required to kindly let them have your full proposal so that they can take it to their boss. This reduces your ability to trade concessions and secure a robust deal. This tactic makes the concessions rather one sided in the other party's favour!

The counter is to insist upon negotiating with the boss directly. If they cannot confirm the value that they will give in return for any concession that you may be prepared to make then you cannot proceed with the negotiation.

"I Need To Get This Approved By Marketing"

A variation on this tactic is to state that some other person or department needs to sign off the agreement. Again, request that in order to conclude the deal to the satisfaction of both parties that the other person joins the negotiation.

Other tricks that you may encounter include:

"Hurry! Hurry!"

You will recall that time can be a factor that affects the power balance in negotiations. The person with the most time generally has the power balance tipped in their favour. If you desperately need to have a deal concluded to hit your year end sales targets, then you are far more likely to make generous concessions than if you had another nine months to hit your sales targets.

In addition, the less time you have to think and plan and prepare the weaker you will be in the negotiation. For this reason, watch out for people who insist that they need to know immediately, or by the following day. They are using the time factor to try to force you into making the concessions they need.

I used to look after a customer who would often call me on a Friday evening at 5pm, tell me that my prices for a high volume product line I supplied had just been undercut by another supplier, and if he didn't have a counterproposal on his desk by 9am on Monday morning then I would lose the business. I either worked over the weekend or lost the business!

I decided to call his bluff and said that I would not be able to offer a counter proposal within the timescale given, and asked him to confirm the new situation in writing as I wanted to release the stock I had allocated to him to another of my customers. After some further discussion he decided to withdraw his threat. I knew and he knew that it was highly unlikely that he would be able to secure sufficient stock of the product line in question from another supplier and that this would interfere with his ability to maintain stock levels in his retail outlets. I could only take this approach because I understood his business in depth, which reinforces the importance of planning and preparing correctly.

"The Hot Potato"

This is a variation on the tactic above. The hot potato is a problem or issue that the other party throws to you. It is, however, not really *your* problem – it is their problem. They are throwing it to you to force you to take some action or make a concession.

I was recently recruiting a new secretary and used a number of employment agencies to find some suitable candidates. After interviewing one of the candidates, my contact from the employment agency phoned me for my decision. I told him that I would be making my final decision the following day when I'd had a chance to fully consider all of the various candidates. He then attempted to toss me a "hot potato" by stating that he had committed to the person he had put forward for interview that they would have a decision that day. Therefore, he had to know my decision immediately.

I declined to catch his hot potato, the promise he had made was his problem and not mine, and I would make my decision when it suited me. I invited him to think about how likely I would be to use his services again if he persisted in trying to force a decision from me and he decided to call me back the following day instead!

Don't catch other people's hot potatoes! A sign above my new secretary's desk says, "A lack of organisation on your part does not constitute a crisis on my part!" I get the message!

"The Salami Slicer"

When you buy salami from the delicatessen the meat is sliced in very thin slices. In a negotiation the other party may attempt to "salami" you by securing a series of what seem to be minor concessions on your part. It is only when the salami slice concessions are viewed in the totality that you realise just how much you have given away! You can counter the salami by using the "If you...Then I" principle with every attempt at taking a slice. Salami back – there's no such thing as a free lunch! Not even Salami!

"The Nibble"

The nibble tactic is used when the negotiation appears to have been concluded. You have shaken hands and (rather like the crowd at the 1966 World Cup final) you think it's all over. You relax and sit back in you chair. In what appears to be an afterthought, perhaps even as you are walking out of the meeting, the other party casually states, "That includes the free warranty, right?" Caught off guard many people will end up agreeing to a minor concession. The Japanese Samurai had a saying: "After victory tighten your helmet straps" – and they were absolutely right.

The counter to the nibble is to politely refuse and to state that you thought the negotiation has concluded and that if the other party wants the free warranty (or whatever) that you will need to revisit the agreement. An alternative approach is to nibble right back!

"Cherry Picking"

This is a tactic where the other party chooses the elements of your proposal that they *do* like, and rejects the elements that they *don't* like. They are cherry picking just the elements that they want. For the deal to work for you, you may need all of the elements included in your proposal. Make sure your positioning is clear – nothing is agreed until everything is agreed.

"Meet me halfway"

This tactic involves asking the other party to "meet me halfway". It appears to be very fair with each party making a concession. However, halfway is not necessarily a good place for you and the other party may have added significant amounts of "padding" (e.g. They have told you that they can't pay any more than £100 per unit when in fact their available budget is up to £200 per unit) to their initial position anyway. A good counter is to thank them for their willingness to move, and then to emphasise the fact that, due to their concession, the gap between where you and they want to conclude is now smaller. Then keep looking for ways to close this now smaller gap!

"Help me out this time and I'll see you right next time"

This is when the other party makes some promise of future benefit to you if you make a concession this time. Unfortunately the benefit you will get is somewhat vague and it is very likely that having set the precedent this time that the same tactic will be applied in the future also. Counter this by only enhancing your proposition to the customer when you receive specific and tangible benefits in return.

"I'm Your Friend"

It is not unknown for someone to encourage you to make a concession by using emotional blackmail. They will use their "friendship" with you to leverage a concession that you would not usually make. Even when I do business with friends – business is business! I wouldn't expect any friend of mine to give me a deal that was not beneficial to them also. I draw a distinction between my friends and being friendly with people that I do business with.

"My Hearing Isn't Very Good"

This tactic is where someone pretends to have misheard you during a negotiation. They will then proceed through the negotiation assuming that what they "misheard" is genuine. Sometimes these erroneous concessions can gather a life of their own. This is another reason why clarifying and summarising regularly are strongly recommended. Don't let any differences of understanding gather momentum. If the other party purposefully mishears what you say, politely and firmly correct them. Once this has been done they will be less likely to repeat this behaviour.

"The False Concession"

This tactic works by getting you to make a concession because you cannot meet a demand from the other party. However, the demand is a work of fiction and its sole purpose is for it to be used to get a concession from the other party. For example, if someone knows that it takes you a week to arrange delivery then they may demand next day delivery. To compensate for your lack of ability to deliver tomorrow you might be tempted to concede on the price of the item being delivered. The other party knows that you can't possibly deliver tomorrow and indeed don't expect or need you to do so. They are only demanding the next day delivery to force a concession from you.

"We Will Send You To The Russian Front"

During World War 2, no-one wanted to be posted to the Russian front. Anywhere was better than being sent to the Russian Front.

This tactic works in the same way. Let us assume that the other party in the negotiation has a proposal that they want you to agree to. For the sake of illustration let's call this Proposal A.

The other party encourages you to accept Proposal A because the alternative (being sent to the Russian Front) is far worse. It is only the contrast between the Russian Front alternative and Proposal A that makes Proposal A seem in any way attractive. Proposal A could be an awful deal for you. The only reason it seems in any way reasonable is when viewed against the Russian Front proposal.

A classic use of the Russian Front tactic is where a company tells a current supplier that they will have to make a 10% reduction in their pricing, or else the company will be "forced" to put the contract out to tender.

Faced with the alternative of losing the business, or at best having to submit a more competitive tender, the supplier may decide to make the price reduction. The 10% price reduction is more attractive than the Russian Front threat of having the contract put out to tender.

A good counter to the Russian Front is firstly to recognise the tactic and secondly to consider the need that lies behind such a request. A company may genuinely need to reduce the cost of the products they are purchasing for re-sale - to make enough profit to survive for example! Behind the request lies a need. The skilled negotiator will want to understand the need and see how they can help the other party get what they want. In return the skilled negotiator gets what they want. Even Russian Front requests can yield significant benefits for the skilled negotiator.

So there you have a downright dirty collection of tricks and tactics. As stated earlier I would strongly advise you to focus on improving your overall skills as a negotiator. This will enable you to negotiate robust and profitable deals far better than using a few manipulative tactics.

It is important to know of these tactics so that you can defend against them. In addition, in one-off transactional negotiations you may wish to use one or more of these tactics. They can be very effective, particularly with inexperienced negotiators. If you do decide to use some of the above tactics though then please ensure you have considered the possible consequences and repercussions.

Happy Negotiating!

So here we are at the end of the book! Along the way we have explored the art and science of negotiating. If you absorb the contents of this book and make it your own then you will have armed yourself with a very valuable life skill – the ability to negotiate.

As I said at the beginning of this book, all the material things you want and haven't got are currently in the hands of someone else. Negotiation will help you get them into your hands!

As I conclude this book I am reminded of the story of the king who ruled a far away land, many hundreds of years ago. The king was an intelligent man who valued knowledge and learning greatly.

He gathered the wisest scholars in his kingdom together and instructed them to gather and collate and condense the greatest wisdom in the world together in one place. After two years they returned with one hundred volumes that contained the greatest wisdom of the ages. After surveying the one hundred books the king announced, "This is good work, but there is far too much for any one man to absorb. Please condense this wisdom down further."

Another year passed and the scholars returned with ten volumes of wisdom. Again the king asked for this wisdom to be condensed still further.

Six months later and the scholars returned with just one volume of wisdom. Still the king felt that this was far too much knowledge and asked it to be condensed even further still.

The scholars returned after a further six months with just one piece of paper. After reading it the king asked them to condense the greatest wisdom of the ages down to just one sentence so that it could easily be shared across his kingdom.

When the scholars returned the king asked them to read the one sentence that contained the greatest wisdom known to man to him. One of the scholars announced to the king, "Your majesty, the greatest wisdom known to man is: *There is no such thing as a free lunch'"

Make this your negotiation motto and you will always make sure that you only ever give when you get something in return. Don't expect free lunches and don't supply them either.

And please remember, what Chester L. Karrass said, "In business you don't get what you deserve, you get what you negotiate."

Learn to be an exceptional negotiator and you will be able to get more of what you want. At the very least your bank balance will improve dramatically!

I hope you get a great deal of benefit from this book and I hope to meet you in person at one of my speeches, or to welcome you as a participant on one of my "Bare Knuckle Selling" or "Bare Knuckle Negotiating" boot camps very soon.

Good Luck and Good Negotiating!

Simon Hazeldine

About The Author

Simon Hazeldine demonstrates his mental focus by walking barefoot over a twenty foot bed of razor sharp broken glass!

Simon Hazeldine MSc, FInstSMM

"...a hard hitting speaker who will give you a wake up call that you'll never forget!"

Simon Hazeldine is a recognised expert in the fields of:

- The Psychology of Performance
- The Psychology of Influence
- Selling and Negotiation

Simon writes a monthly column on the psychology of performance in four national magazines and is the author of:

"Bare Knuckle Selling", "Bare Knuckle Negotiation", "The Winner's Edge: Psychological Strategies for Exceptional Performance" and a series of eight psychological training guides for martial artists and sportspeople.

Simon works internationally as a speaker, trainer, coach and facilitator in the areas of performance, leadership, sales, negotiation and influential communication.

His "High Performance Coaching Skills", "Group Training Techniques" and "Negotiation Skills" programmes are currently being used in 28 countries around the world.

Simon has a Masters Degree in the psychology and management of performance. In addition he is Certified as a Master Practitioner and Trainer of NLP, and is a Fellow of the Institute of Sales and Marketing Management.

Simon has extensive experience in sales both in the UK and abroad and has been responsible for numerous client accounts each worth in excess of £20 million in sales. Prior to his career as a trainer and speaker Simon provided event security and personal protection services to celebrities in the television and music industry.

Simon Hazeldine's acclaimed keynote speeches include:

"How To Raise Your Game", "How To Get What You Want By Being Selfish and Unreasonable", "Are You Tough Enough? - The 7 Secrets of Mental Toughness", "How To Find Your Customers G-Spot", "How To Hurt Your Competitors Using Bare Knuckle Selling"

Learn more at:
Email: www.simonhazeldine.com

Bibliography

Covey, Stephen, *The Seven Habits Of Highly Effective People*, Simon & Schuster, 1999

Kennedy, Gavin, *Everything Is Negotiable*, Hutchinson Business Books, 1989

Fisher, Roger/Ury,William/Patton, Bruce, *Getting to Yes*, Business Books Limited, 1991

Forsyth, Patrick, *The Negotiators Pocketbook*, Management Pocketbooks, 1993

Greene, Robert, *The 48 Laws Of Power*, Profile Books, 2000

Hazeldine, Simon, *Bare Knuckle Selling*, Lean Marketing Press, 2005

Hazeldine, Simon, *The Winner's Edge*, Winners Edge Publications, 2004

Lakhani, Dave, *Persuasion: The Art Of Getting What You Want*, Wiley, 2005

McCormick, Mark H, *Success Secrets*, Fontana, 1989

McCormick, Mark H, *What They Don't Teach You At Harvard Business School*, Collins, 1984

Mushashi, Miyamoto, *A Book Of Five Rings*, Allison & Busby, 1974

Nierenberg, Gerard, *The Complete Negotiator*, Nierneberg and Zeif Piblications, 1986

Tzu, Sun, *The Art Of War*, Wordsworth Reference, 1993

Ury, William, *Getting Past No*, Business Books Limited, 1991

Yuan, Gao, *Lure The Tiger Out Of The Mountains: How To Apply The 36 Strategems Of Ancient China To The Modern World*, Piatkus, 1991

Dawson, Roger, *The Secrets Of Power Negotiating*, Nightingale Conant, 1997

Want Some More?

**Book Simon Hazeldine as a Keynote Speaker
for your Conference or Event**

*"...a hard hitting speaker who will give you a
wake up call that you'll never forget!"*

Keynote speeches include:

* *"How to get what you want by being selfish and unreasonable"*
* *"How to hurt your competitors with Bare Knuckle Selling"*
* *"How to raise your game"*
* *"Are you tough enough? The 7 secrets of mental toughness"*

Further information on Simon's keynote speeches can be obtained from his Professional Speakers Association webpage:

www.simonhazeldine.com

E3 Group: Inspiring and Enabling Exceptional Performance

*"The E3 Group provides consultancy and training that delivers
significant sales and business performance enhancement"*

The unique E3 Group approach is based on ensuring that you have the three essential factors that guarantee on-going sales success hard-wired into your organisation.

Highly effective solutions will be specifically designed, tailored and delivered in house to meet your specific requirements.

Examples of training solutions provided by the E3 Group include:

* Sales Skills Training
* Advanced Sales Skills Training
* Negotiation Skills Training
* Cold Calling Skills Training
* Coaching Skills for Managers and Leaders
* Effective Sales Management
* Effective Performance Management
* Developing Superior Customer Relationships

- Selling with ...
- The Psychology of Per... ...nce
- Key Account Management and ... Account Management training
- Public Speaking and Presentation Skills
- The Psychology of Exceptional Performance
- Developing Mental Toughness
- Performance Leadership

The E3 Group also offers a series of open programmes:

- **The Bare Knuckle Selling Bootcamp:** 2 day open programme that will teach you how to be a bare knuckle seller!

- **The Bare Knuckle Negotiation Bootcamp:** 2 day open programme that will give you the winning edge

- **Advanced Selling Workshop:** 2 day open programme on the psychology of persuasion and influence

- **Psychology of Performance Workshop:** 2 day open programme that will reveal the real psychological strategies and techniques used by elite performers

- **I Will!:** 1 day motivation and peak performance seminar with Simon Hazeldine. Break through limiting beliefs, take control of your life, discover your simple single truth and raise your game to new heights.

To book Simon as your speaker or to find out more about E3 Group's services and courses contact Simon Hazeldine:

The E3 Group
1 Dexter Close
Quorn
Loughborough
Leicestershire
LE12 8EH
United Kingdom

www.simonhazeldine.com

GET YOUR EXCLUSIVE 'BARE KNUCKLE' BONUSES

To download your FREE and exclusive 'Bare Knuckle' bonuses, designed to help you further build on your persuasive powers, visit the link below and complete the form.

Get your FREEBIES now at...

www.BookShaker.com/bareknuckle

BARE KNUCKLE
SELLING

KNOCKOUT SALES TACTICS THEY WON'T TEACH YOU AT BUSINESS SCHOOL

SIMON HAZELDINE
FOREWORD BY DR. JOE VITALE